GHOS— —ND LEGENDS OF NORTHEAST SOUTH DAKOTA

DEBORAH A. CUYLE

Haunted America

Published by Haunted America
A Division of The History Press
Charleston, SC
www.historypress.com

First published 2024

Manufactured in the United States

ISBN 9781467156684

Library of Congress Control Number: 2024936785

Notice: The information in this book is true and complete to the best of our knowledge. It is offered without guarantee on the part of the author or The History Press. The author and The History Press disclaim all liability in connection with the use of this book.

I dedicate this book to all my friends, my family and the wonderful team at Arcadia Publishing and The History Press. My love of history, writing and haunted places is ultimately fueled by their continued interest and support as I travel my way through the various states.

My appreciation also goes out to all my spiritual BFFs who have joined me in a little ghost hunting now and then and have helped me pursue my paranormal research and beliefs. An open mind is an open door. I personally have experienced so many things I cannot explain that I can no longer even remotely doubt the existence of ghosts or spirits.

I am currently living in a crumbling mansion built in 1883 (which is also a former funeral home), and I am discovering there are spirits everywhere—if we only take notice and pay attention to their small signals, their signs… Their whispers.

We seem to have several friendly spirits entertaining us in this old house. A thin woman who wears a long, black dress. A cheerful gentleman who is very considerate and helpful. A male jokester who likes to mock me calling for my cat…

So I also dedicate this book to all the active and interesting ghosts out there. Without you, my books would not be possible!

Happy ghost hunting, y'all!

CONTENTS

PREFACE

In this book, I explore new avenues for hauntings, paranormal realms and mysterious places. Over the years, I have learned there is so much more to the strange happenings we experience than just ghostly apparitions and things that go bump in the night! Many unique, unexplained and unusual things can haunt us—as an example, the baffling odor of a perfume or cigar smoke once linked to a loved one that somehow materializes when one is thinking about that deceased person. Is it a sign that the spirit of that person is trying to communicate? Or is it simply a bizarre coincidence?

The smell of a special fragrance a loved one wore while alive that has long since been discontinued—where is it coming from? How exactly do spirits create odors? Or are the odors a figment of our imagination, fabricated by the yearning hope that our loved ones are still with us?

I often smell cigarette smoke when no one is smoking. Is it my mother (who loved to smoke) somehow letting me know she is still here with me?

As is common with my books, I have tried to incorporate into each chapter as many historical facts, names and dates as possible. I feel this brings the ghosts and their stories to life and also makes learning about the different towns more interesting. Many of my readers tell me they enjoy both— learning about the town's history while reading about the ghosts that haunt it. I love hearing a good ghost story and then, on researching the building, actually being able to find evidence of someone with the spirit's name who actually lived there (or died there) at one time or another.

There are so many strange happenings in the world—bizarre phenomena and things that defy logic. There are fantastic places, monsters, unsolved mysteries, lost legends and more that intrigue and delight us!

Being a near death experience survivor, I am a little more open-minded than most people. In 2010, I had a horrible accident at the hospital: I was overdosed, which ultimately led to my demise. The staff was eventually able to revive me, but the lack of oxygen left me with some mental difficulties. After much hard work and determination, I am now able to function somewhat normally (although I do still have problems that arise from the brain injury).

My dying somehow opened up to me doors into the paranormal world. I began to experience things I could not explain, and it was difficult to determine whether what I was experiencing was due to the brain injury or coming from another dimension. This proved incredibly stressful and tiring to me. Eventually, I was able to understand things better and evaluate each experience for what it was.

People soon began asking me to contact their deceased loved ones (which I did, but it always left me with blinding headaches). Although the messages and information that would come though from the dead were extremely accurate, the process left me exhausted, so I chose not to do it anymore. Curious individuals or persons grieving were always so excited about hearing from the other side, but sometimes they were more interested in "proving" me right or wrong. It was not worth it.

But these readings did prove to *me* that there definitely is another dimension after we die, and deceased people can still communicate with the living. There is no doubt whatsoever in my mind that ghosts exist. Now, what *does* still baffle me is how and why they exist. Why do some people choose to remain in the Earth realm after they die instead of moving on to heaven? What messages do they seek to reveal? What unsolved problem do they wish to resolve? Murder victims and suicides have the highest rate of ghostly activity. In this book, I address many murders and the restless spirits that are hanging around seeking justice or resolution.

Maybe, someday, science can prove what really happens to us after we die—the eternal mystery questioned by every living being—but until the riddle is solved, it is all just speculation. Religion and science may someday agree, but it's more likely they will not. I see both sides of the debate. Too many unexplained things happen to each of us for us *not* to entertain the idea of ghosts and the spirit world. I read somewhere that God or spirits do give us signs when we ask for them, but we as humans are too busy or too close-minded to see them or recognize them for what they are. I often wonder what life would be like if people were not so skeptical about the possibility of the spirit world. How would that change the way people behave in this world today? Would this be reassuring or terrifying to most people? I am often baffled by people who tell me that they believe in the afterlife but not in spirits. How can the two really be separated? Perhaps some dead people just choose to haunt a place while other spirits choose not to? It's a wonderful mystery.

I have great interest in and respect for the early pioneers, a fascination with local history and a personal passion for old buildings. I love all the lore, legends and ghost and spirit stories people have told me. It is fun to walk the same streets today—the same ones early settlers once walked—and think about how it was in the old days. When I look at old brick buildings or original hardwood floors, I try to imagine the thousands of people who once walked these streets or visited these buildings, the horses that pulled wagons and goods, the gunslingers and outlaws, the bartenders and shopkeepers, all of them living their lives and going about their business, just as we all do today. I would have loved to have been alive in the late 1800s.

Many of these people would now be lost to the world, nothing more than a mere mention in the newspaper, if not remembered and shared through stories. I think including their true-life stories here, even if tragic, keeps their memory alive—and possibly, people can learn from their mistakes or experiences when they read about them.

Ghost stories, legends and folklore exist in every town, big and small, new and old. Human beings are fascinated by the afterlife and are eager to somehow capture proof of the spirit world. But what are these spirits that people are so eager to find proof of? Apparitions and odors are the most common forms of paranormal activity, although it's impossible to "capture" odors and prove their existence. Strange noises are also common forms of paranormal activity. These noises often imitate environmental sounds or the sounds of animal or human activities, such as crying and moaning, but they can also imitate the sounds of chairs moving or dishes breaking. Paranormal activity can also come in the form of a crisis apparition (paranormal activity created by a traumatic incident, such as murder or the like) or the appearance of a passed loved one offering comfort. These are onetime events that typically occur when a living person is undergoing a personal crisis. Unfortunately, these crisis apparitions are commonly shrugged off as daydreams or ignored and labeled as strange events caused by personal stress.

However, I would like my readers to keep in mind how much energy it takes for a spirit to manifest itself. It is an extremely hard task, so it is particularly important that the spirit is acknowledged and given words of thanks. While single instances of paranormal activity are exciting, the apparition of an animal or a person is only considered a haunting when it continues to appear in the same location multiple times.

Within the walls of old buildings remains the residual energy needed to keep their spirits restless and their stories alive—and hopefully their ghostly apparitions seen today.

History is full of people who haunt us, who want to be recognized and never forgotten for what they accomplished while alive—the improvements they created for a town or what they offered their family and community. This book is about those fascinating spirits: the spirited people who were part of the places in *Ghosts and Legends of Northeast South Dakota*. Hauntings can come in many shapes and forms; anything that frightens us can haunt us!

Most of the stories in this book were told to me by locals, and some have been pulled from old newspapers—all told out of fun and for the love of history, ghost stories, legends and lore. This book is *not* intended to be a nonfiction project, and even after hundreds of hours hunched over reading and researching, I still find conflicting dates, misspelled names and inconsistent historic details—so please take it for what it is. I tried to be as accurate as possible, but this is mostly a book full of tales of many mischievous ghosts and the interesting history of northeast South Dakota. Enjoy!

ACKNOWLEDGEMENTS

T here are many people to thank for this endeavor, and without their help and guidance, this book would not have been possible. My wonderful editor, Artie Crisp, is always such a pleasure to work with, along with all the other incredible people at Arcadia Publishing and The History Press. Their enthusiasm for their mission to promote local history is infectious, and I am blessed to work on my books with them. Their dedication to recording local history is nothing less than amazing, and without them, many books would never be written.

I also extend my appreciation to all those who took the time to share with me their personal ghost stories and experiences. Without them, this book would not have the extra flair that I love so much!

And as always, I want to thank every single person who does what they can to preserve history—whether it is volunteering at the local historical society, maintaining old cemeteries and gravestones that otherwise would get neglected or simply researching their private genealogy through sites like Ancestry.com. In this fast-paced and high-tech world, the past can, unfortunately, be forgotten, and every effort to maintain and record valuable data, photographs, diaries, documents, and records is of the utmost importance for future generations.

ONE FINAL REQUEST: PLEASE do not disturb or trespass on any of the locations listed throughout this book. To explore or investigate any locations, please acquire permission from the property or business owners. Although some of the buildings in *Ghosts and Legends of Northeast South Dakota* no longer exist, the energy left behind by tragedy, murder or unsolved crime does linger. Please take only photographs back with you so the next person can have the same experience as you. Thank you for understanding.

South Dakota

ONE OF THE MOST HAUNTED PLACES IN THE UNITED STATES

Ghosts are history demanding to be heard, and we are the ears that can hear it.
—*John Burnside*

GHOSTS. A single word that immediately conjures up all sorts of images and ideas. Hauntings and ghostly spirits have been around as long as humans and evoke every emotion from fear to intrigue to refusal to believe. Every culture treats death and the spirit world differently—different rituals, customs and burial practices—but all have one thing in common: the afterlife.

Ghosts are often considered to be supernatural entities or the spirits of deceased individuals that are believed to exist in an odd state between the physical world and the afterlife. People have different interpretations of what ghosts really are and how they interact with the living world. Some common beliefs associated with ghosts include:

APPARITIONS: Ghosts are often described as appearing in a transparent or misty form and/or as orbs. When they choose to, they can be seen, heard or felt by living individuals.

UNFINISHED BUSINESS: One common belief is that ghosts linger in the mortal realm due to unresolved issues or unfinished business. They may be seeking closure, redemption or revenge for past actions or for things that transpired while they were alive.

HAUNTINGS: Ghosts are often associated with haunted locations where they are believed to manifest as repeated phenomena, such as strange sounds, unexplained odors, movements or visual apparitions. These occurrences are attempts by the spirits to communicate with the living.

EMOTIONAL ATTACHMENTS: Some paranormal investigators believe that strong emotions, such as intense fear, love, hate or even serious trauma, can anchor a spirit to the physical world, leading to its presence as a ghost.

GUIDANCE OR PROTECTION: Some believe ghosts act as protective or guiding spirits for their living descendants or friends. They might offer advice, warn of danger or lovingly watch over family members to keep them safe and sound.

Ghost stories, legends and folklore exist in every town—big and small, new and old—as human beings are eager to capture proof of the spirit world. Apparitions are the most common form of paranormal activity. The spirit of an animal or a person that keeps reappearing at a location over and over again is classified as an "actual" haunting. An important characteristic of a actual haunting is noise. These frightening noises imitate the sounds of human and animal activities, such as crying or laughter, chairs moving, dishes breaking, cats meowing or dogs barking.

Another form of activity is called the "crisis apparition." These paranormal events typically occur when a living person undergoes a crisis and the spirit of a loved one appears to offer them comfort.

Some people believe that environmental factors, such as infrasound or sound waves at frequencies lower than the normal human hearing range, will cause feelings of unease, anxiety and even visual hallucinations that can often be mistaken for ghostly activity. But what is the real truth?

It is also believed that ghosts are the "confused dead." For some reason, they do not understand that they are dead and thus wander around restlessly. Ghosts may also cling to the earthly world because they need something resolved. Was their killer captured and sentenced? Is there a valuable or money that the ghost wants to make sure gets in the right hands? Or were their possessions distributed in a manner that went against their final wishes. Ghosts linger for many reasons.

Spirit guides, on the other hand, are aware they are dead but still wish to communicate with the living. They can connect with those who can listen to them, offering positive advice and helpful information.

In *Ghosts and Legends of Northeast South Dakota*, we will explore a large variety of paranormal activities, gruesome true crimes, creepy happenings, unexplained events and much more! What kinds of things scare you?

I hope the stories in these pages make the hair on the back of your neck stand up and that this will be followed by a faint whisper from someone unseen or maybe the touch of an invisible hand…

CHAPTER 1
PIONEERS AND HAUNTED HISTORIC BUILDINGS

Ghosts are whispers of the stories that have left their mark
on the places and people we love.
—Unknown

B efore we dive into the creepier side of northeast South Dakota, let us explore a little bit about its interesting past.

South Dakota's fascinating history begins with the presence of several Indigenous peoples, including the Lakota Sioux, Dakota Sioux, Nakota Sioux and many other tribes. In the 1800s, hundreds of settlers began taking over the land, hoping to strike it rich one way or another. Many others were busy filing land claims and marking their territory. Other pioneers were not so responsible and productive, so they resorted to stealing and bribery.

To cater to the influx of early American pioneers taking over the Natives' land, the United States government negotiated treaties with the tribes. When their promises went unfulfilled, the Native Americans became incredibly angry and hostile toward the people moving onto their land, and they began feeling like they had been taken advantage of.

Tensions finally boiled over, and in June 1876, the Battle of Little Bighorn ensued. During the bloody two-day battle, up to 100 Native Americans from the Lakota Sioux and Cheyenne tribes (led by leaders such as Sitting Bull and Crazy Horse) were killed, and approximately 276 soldiers from the United States Seventh Cavalry Regiment lost their lives. This bloodbath is

The ghosts of the hundreds of men who lost their lives in 1876, during Custer's Last Stand, haunt the land where the battle took place. *Courtesy of Zonnieboy, October 1994, via Creative Commons.*

commonly referred to as Custer's Last Stand because it resulted in the defeat and death of Lieutenant Colonel George Armstrong Custer, who was killed along with every soldier of the five companies he led.

They say the prairie where the battle took place is littered with the ghosts of these poor men. The negative energy created by this battle still resonates in the soil. The graves mark the spots where the bodies once lay in a gruesome reminder of how many men (and horses) tragically lost their lives.

South Dakota continued to grow at a rapid pace. In 1889, South Dakota was admitted as the fortieth state of the United States of America. The citizens decided they needed a governor. The governor is responsible for enforcing state laws and maintaining law and order within the state. And they felt they knew just the right guy for the job.

Arthur Calvin Mellette (1842–1896) was elected the first governor of South Dakota in 1889. (He was also the last governor of Dakota Territory.) That was the same year President Benjamin Harrison signed the proclamation making South Dakota the fortieth state. Mellette was a prominent and well-respected figure in South Dakota, and citizens were proud to have such a man in charge of their state. Born on June 23, 1842, in Henry County, Indiana, Mellette moved to Dakota Territory in the 1870s and quickly

Left: Arthur Mellette, South Dakota's first governor, moved to Dakota Territory in the 1870s and quickly became involved in local politics. *Courtesy of Library of Congress (LOC), Highsmith, Carol M, photographer, #2021757523.*

Below: Arthur Mellette built a beautiful mansion in Watertown for his wife and four sons in 1885. It is now a well-preserved museum. *Courtesy of author.*

became involved in local politics. He met his love, Margaret Wylie (1843–1938), when he rented a room at her family's home in Bloomington, Indiana.

When Watertown was little more than a few sparse buildings, Mellette decided to build a camp down on Lake Kampeska. The family lived there until they could afford to build the beautiful mansion on Prospect Hill in town. Construction began in 1885 on what was to be the private residence of Mr. Mellette and his family: his wife, Margaret Wylie, and his four sons: Theopholis Wylie, Charles Edmond (1869–1964), Arthur Anton (1872–1953) and Joshua Richard (1872–1929).

The Mellettes continued to enjoy their home in Watertown until 1895, when other callings led them (in what they thought was a temporary move) to Pittsburg, Kansas. Unfortunately, Arthur Mellette died on May 25, 1896, of a heart attack while visiting his daughter in Pittsburg. His body was sent back to Watertown and interred in Mount Hope Cemetery. After the death of her husband, Margaret continued to live in Pittsburg with her son Anton until her death at age ninety-five on November 29, 1938.

Although the beautiful Mellette mansion in Watertown is *not* reported to be haunted, it does offer an excellent insight into the masonry and construction during that period and excellent examples of household arrangements of the time and how the Mellette family lived. The amazing spiral staircase that leads from the main floor up to the third floor is testament to the craftsmanship and attention to detail used by carpenters during the late 1800s.

The home is now a beautifully restored museum open to the public for tours. The Mellette House stands as a legacy of the early history of South Dakota and the important individuals who helped it become the lovely state it is today.

NOTE: The Mellette House is located at 421 5th Avenue NW, Watertown, SD 57201.

THE GHOSTS OF FORT SISSETON

A ghost story from Mike D.:

> *When I was visiting Fort Sisseton, I felt as though I was being watched all the time, but no one was there. I have heard many rumors of the fort being haunted by an old soldier. I wondered who this soldier was. Did he get killed*

on the property? I did not actually see the ghost soldier, but I certainly felt the hair on the back of my neck stand up a few times for no reason!

One of the eeriest places found in northeast South Dakota is old Fort Sisseton. Tales of sightings of the ghosts of a little boy, a former servant and an old buffalo soldier abound. Many of the employees have incredible, true-life ghost stories to share. Fort Sisseton is the oldest building in northeast South Dakota and is located near Lake City, South Dakota. It was established in 1864 and played a significant role in the region's history during the horrific Indian Wars.

Built in 1864, the thirty-five-acre park has a plentiful history of strange stories and weird events. The haunted grounds originally cost $500,000 to construct. It included two three-hundred-foot-long barracks, a hospital, clay ovens for baking, a parade ground and another nineteen buildings. The fort was conveniently situated twenty miles from the Britton Railway Station. Originally, the fort was built to protect the early settlers from the hostile Natives who were attacking and killing them. The Santee Sioux were angry at the White men due to broken promises and their sacred land being taken from them without permission.

The Fort Sisseton commander's house has a female ghost who burns phantom bedbugs off the walls. *Courtesy of LOC, Charles E., photographer, 1933, # sd0016.*

The fort served the United States Army from 1864 to 1889, housing calvary and infantry soldiers. Originally named Fort Wadsworth (after Brigadier General Samuel Wadsworth), it was renamed Fort Sisseton in August 1876 after the nearby Sisseton tribe. (*Sisi-tonwan* means "Fish Village.")

The fort was abandoned as an active military post in 1889. By the late nineteenth century, the Indian Wars were largely over, and the military focus had shifted away from frontier forts to more important locations.

In the 1900s, the fort became a working cattle ranch owned by the Wellman family—specifically, Colonel Josiah "Joe" Wellman, a Civil War veteran and entrepreneur. Over time, the old military structures were repurposed by the Wellmans for housing ranch workers, storing equipment and other agricultural uses.

In the 1930s, during the Great Depression, the former fort was transformed into a Works Progress Administration camp. Homeless transients were housed at the fort for free in exchange for repairing the neglected buildings. By 1934, over 150 men were living at Fort Sisseton and hard at work fixing up the place. The buildings were in desperate need of repairs and upgrades, and many people felt they were not even habitable. Large army tents, complete with stoves, were assembled near the north barracks to accommodate the men. New roofs, new foundations and wooden floors were slowly completed at the fort. The abandoned officers' quarters, the commander's quarters and the hospital also received extensive remodeling.

The fort property has some interesting architectural features. The old barn had forty-foot rafters, which implies that there were very large trees on the site at one time. An odd coincidence is that lightning struck the northwest corner of the officer's quarters two times—in the exact same spot!

One of the men to remember from the fort's history is the hardworking doctor who went out of his way to administer medicine and provide valuable health insights to the workers. Without missing a beat, Doctor D.B. Rice from Britton, South Dakota, made his regular rounds to the fort to keep the men healthy. Even so, one winter, a man died. Since his demise was during a brutal snowstorm, the ground was frozen, and his body had to be stored in a cold room for eight days before it could be buried. Is this man one of the ghosts that haunts the fort?

In 1959, the site became a designated state park. In the 1990s, it was transformed again, into a workplace for prisoners.

A GRISLY TALE SURROUNDS the old "hanging tree" at the fort. Oddly, this tree also had a large dinner bell fastened between two of the largest limbs. The tale describes two AWOL (absent without leave) African American soldiers who were hanged from the tree until they were dead as punishment for their crimes. The officers left the bodies there for several days for others to view as a brutal warning. Some say they have seen the men's ghostly figures near the hanging tree. Do the spirits of the mistreated men linger because they wish to seek revenge on their killers? No records can be found disclosing the names of the hanged men.

Today, the appearance of strange lights, the feeling of being touched by invisible hands and countless sightings of full-body apparitions are not uncommon at Fort Sisseton. Currently, the fort is reportedly host to three very active ghosts. The Lady in White is often seen peering out from the upstairs window of the house on the site. She is always wearing a white nightgown, similar to the ones servants used to wear during that era. During the 1870s, the fort was struggling with an extreme bedbug infestation. The bugs were so bad that female workers had to burn them off the walls every night before the men could go to bed. The women would hold their candles

Many buildings like these barracks at Fort Sisseton are haunted. The property has three active ghosts. *Courtesy of LOC, Historic American Buildings Survey, Creator, and Charles E Peterson, 1933, #sd0004.*

dangerously close to the walls so the heat from the flames would kill the bugs. The insects would then fall to the floor to be swept up by the thousands and tossed outside.

The Lady in White is often seen carrying a candle. Who is this mysterious lady? Why does she refuse to end her horrible nightly job of killing the bedbugs? No one knows.

The second ghost that haunts the grounds is a little boy. He likes to play with other children when they visit the property. He can often be felt tugging at pant legs and clothes to get the attention of those around him. Once, a prisoner was using an old pay phone when he felt a hard tug on his pant leg. Turning around, he saw the ghostly apparition of the little boy. Did this boy die somehow on the property? Who is he? Who were his parents? No one knows the answers to these questions or why his spirit chooses to hang around the fort.

The third apparition frequently seen by employees and tourists is the ghost of a buffalo soldier. It is believed that this ghost is that of an African American man named J.C. Smith, of the Company D Twenty-Fifth Regiment Colored Infantry. Smith worked on the construction of many of the buildings that still stand today, including the guardhouse, where he etched his name on the wall. As a ghost, he likes to tap unsuspecting people on the shoulder to get their attention. He was also often seen by the old pay phone. Why does Smith choose to haunt the fort? Does he have a mysterious story to tell? Does he have a secret burning inside him that he wishes someone would uncover?

The Twenty-Fifth Colored Infantry Regiment was begun in January 1864 and recruited many African American men from all over the United States. They became known as the buffalo soldiers—some say because when their hair was shaved short, it resembled the hide of a buffalo. These valuable units were created to help maintain order in several states of the western frontier. Their orders were to protect settlers and railroad crews and engage in various military campaigns against hostile Native American tribes.

In 1880, the buffalo soldiers were sent off to protect the Dakota Territory.

Research has shown a James Smith in the United States Colored Troops Military Service Records from 1864 to 1865 who served in the Twenty-Fifth Infantry, proving his existence. The fort served the United States Army from

An unidentified Twenty-Fifth Infantry, Company D buffalo soldier poses for his picture in 1884. *Courtesy of LOC, Goff, O.S., photographer, #2010645137.*

Left: A war card from 1864 proving a J. Smith was stationed at Fort Sisseton. He now haunts the grounds. *Courtesy of U.S. Colored Troops Military Service Records, 1863–65, Twenty-Fifth Infantry.*

Below: A group of unidentified buffalo soldiers of the Twenty-Fifth Infantry in 1890, some wearing buffalo robes. *Courtesy of LOC, #3g06161.*

1864 to 1889, housing calvary and infantry soldiers; Smith would have been stationed there the first year the fort opened.

Why would Smith still be hanging around the fort after almost 160 years? Rumor states that Smith was later sentenced to death elsewhere, but records have not been found to prove this tale. So why does Smith continue to haunt the old fort? Did he scratch his name on the wall of the guardhouse knowing he would eventually come back to haunt the building after he died? The reason for Smith's ghostly actions continues to remain a mystery.

Today, the Civil War–era fort has been beautifully preserved and boasts fourteen of its original twenty-two buildings; it also has a wonderful museum and great camping sites. People come from all over to enjoy outdoor water sports and family-friendly events (including haunted ones!), watch war reenactments and explore the visitor center, gift shop and much more.

The city of Sisseton originated in 1892, when $800 could buy you 320 acres of government land. The first year, there were no telephones or telegraphs, of course, and no railroad serviced the town until 1893. There was mud everywhere because there were no sidewalks, either. Native teepees were scattered across the prairie. By 1900, the population of Sisseton had grown to one thousand residents. Today, about 2,459 people call Sisseton home.

NOTE: Fort Sisseton Historic State Park is located at 11907 434th Avenue, Lake City, SD, 57247.
Telephone: (605) 448-5474
Email: fortsisseton@state.sd.us

ABERDEEN

The town of Aberdeen was founded in 1881 when the Milwaukee Railroad extended its line into the Dakota Territory. Why was the little town in South Dakota named after a town in Scotland?

Alexander Mitchell was a prominent businessman and politician and an influential figure in the development of the Milwaukee Railroad, which played a vital role in the growth of Aberdeen, South Dakota, in the late nineteenth century. Mitchell (who was of Scottish descent) had fond memories of Aberdeen, Scotland, and wanted to link his future to his past. It was also a frequent practice in the old days to give new and emerging towns the well-known and recognizable names of larger, more established cities.

In 1883, as the town grew, the Northern State Normal School (now known as Northern State University) was constructed. This also led to an increase in the need for more local libraries and schools. Many historical homes and buildings remain standing in Aberdeen. Today, Aberdeen is home to almost thirty thousand residents. The city continues to expand and increase its business and rural communities and strives to preserve its rich history.

Easton Castle

One of the most spectacular houses in Aberdeen, South Dakota, is called Easton Castle. It is reportedly haunted by the ghost of a female spirit and, possibly, a few partygoers from the 1920s. Others close to the home, however, do not share the belief that it is haunted. Perhaps they choose to ignore the restless spirits? Or maybe some people just want to believe the castle is haunted?

The magnificent mansion was built in 1888 by Charles Sumner Bliss, who was born on November 12, 1867, in Little Valley, New York. He attended Cornell University, in Ithaca, upstate New York, where he studied electrical engineering. His education laid the foundation for his later work in the very early days of computing. Bliss is best known for his work on tabulating machines, which used punched cards and mechanical instruments to perform calculations and record information.

Bliss called his elegant home O-TE-LA after his three daughters: Olive, Tessie and Laura. He combined the first one or two letters of each daughter's name to create the unique and distinctive name for his mansion, a way for Bliss to personally honor and celebrate his family within the walls of their grand residence.

The huge twenty-two-room Queen Anne Victorian is surrounded by twenty gorgeous acres of land. O-TE-LA's exterior was done in yellow brick. The mansion's design is often described as eclectic, featuring a blend of architectural styles, including elements of Romanesque Revival and other influences. One of the notable features of the mansion is its multiple towers and turrets that rise above the building's main structure.

Bliss enjoyed keeping busy, so he also worked as the proprietor of the local seventy-five-room Artesian Hotel. He was also associated with the Bliss-Esler Manufacturing Company, which was based in Aberdeen.

The Blisses were prone to giving lavish parties, which included many prominent guests. One such guest was the famous American children's author L. Frank Baum (1856–1919) and his wife, Maud. Baum wrote *The Wonderful Wizard of Oz*, among many other novels, poems and scripts. While living in Aberdeen from 1888 to 1891, Baum was a frequent guest at the Bliss family home. Baum's niece Leslie Gage (who was the inspiration for Dorothy Gale, the main female character in the *Wonderful Wizard of Oz*) worked for the Blisses as a housekeeper. The *Oz* character, Dorothy, was named after a niece who died: Dorothy Gage, who was the infant niece of Baum's wife. Dorothy Gage died at only five months old in November

The beautiful Easton castle in Aberdeen is haunted by the spirit of Leslie Gage. *Courtesy of Joel Bradshaw, via Creative Commons.*

1898, right as Baum was writing *The Wonderful Wizard of Oz*. The older *Oz* character Dorothy was Baum's tribute to the lost baby girl. It is said Baum wanted to honor the child's "unrealized potential" through his writing.

When Baum met Maud Gage (1861–1953), his cousin's roommate at the time, the pair fell instantly in love. When Baum first set eyes on Maud, he said, "Consider yourself loved, Miss Gage!" They were married just months later.

Baum and Maud owned a local store called Baum's Bazaar in Aberdeen, which did not prosper. Suffering some financial difficulties, Baum began working for the newspaper to make ends meet. Maud's mother, Matilda Gage, also lived with them while in Aberdeen.

Baum continued to write in spite of his financial hardships. The Baums moved to Chicago, Illinois, where he continued working as a newspaper reporter. He never waivered from his faith that his Oz book would be a smash. And his hard work paid off. *The Wonderful Wizard of Oz* was published on May 17, 1900, and was an immediate hit with the public. Baum's financial woes were over. The story was the first fantasy written by an American to

Frank Baum, author of *The Wonderful Wizard of Oz*, in 1911. *Courtesy of* Los Angeles Times, *photographer George Steckel.*

become so successful. The publisher, George M. Hill Company, printed the first edition at a total of ten thousand copies, which quickly sold out. By 1956, the book had sold more than three million copies. Baum later got paid $750,000 for the rights to adapt his book to the silver screen.

Baum moved to Los Angeles, California, after his success. He died peacefully at age sixty-two on May 5, 1919, in his Los Angeles home. Baum had suffered from a heart attack when he was only fourteen years old. His final words were, "Now we can cross the Shifting Sands."

Elegant O-TE-LA would soon become home to another family. Carroll Francis Easton (1857–1935), purchased the home from Bliss in 1892, when Bliss was experiencing financial woes. Both bankers from New York, they easily understood and sympathized with money problems. Easton quickly began remodeling the castle for his wife, Eva (1858–1944); their two daughters, Violet (1888–1958) and Hazel (1890–1918); and son, Russel (1884–1964). The forest around the home was started by Easton himself, as he was an avid tree lover. In 1906, he gleefully gave away free trees to anyone in town who would plant one. He even gave little saplings to schools for free, hoping the children would plant them on Arbor Day. Some credit the development of the current forested land from the once drought-riddled, flat lands of South Dakota in the early 1900s to Easton's passion for planting trees.

As for the Easton family, Hazel died young at age twenty-eight. Carroll Easton died in 1935. Eva Easton died ten years later, in 1945. Violet died in 1958 while living in Virginia. The last living Easton decedent, Russel Easton, continued to live in the castle as a lonely recluse after his mom died. The large estate fall into disrepair until Russel died in 1965.

The neglected mansion was scheduled for demolition. A veterinarian, Dr. Sam Holman, fell in love with the home and purchased it in 1967. The Holman family lovingly restored the mansion to its former glory. Sam's daughters, Tandy and Margaret, now tend to the home and are continually active in preserving the home and surrounding forest.

So why do people believe L. Frank Baum's niece Leslie Gage is the female ghost haunting the third floor of the Easton mansion? Her uncle applied her personal characteristics to the Dorothy character in the *Oz* books, so who knows—maybe it was just a fun place to visit with her uncle while they were alive.

No one really knows why one ghost haunts a certain place or another. Perhaps there was a secret incident that an individual held particularly close while they were alive? This will always be one of the world's greatest mysteries!

NOTE: The Easton Castle is currently being restored and is privately owned, but as of this writing, tours and camping are offered at the site.

WATERTOWN

Watertown's history begins with its founding in 1879 by John E. Kemp, a frontiersman and businessman. The town was located along the Chicago and Northwestern Railroad line, which quickly expanded its growth. The town was also conveniently nestled near the Big Sioux River and Lake Kampeska, both offering good opportunities for traveling and prolific fishing.

In the late 1880s, the population of Watertown was only 746 citizens, but it quickly grew. Today, the population is about 24,000. Watertown continues to enhance its downtown development while preserving many of its historic homes, districts and buildings.

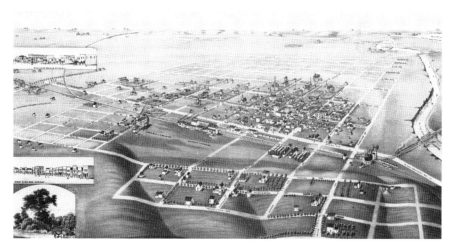

A bird's-eye view of downtown Watertown in 1883. *Courtesy of LOC #75696576, Stoner, J.J. and Beck & Pauli.*

Some wonderful attractions you can enjoy while touring Watertown in search of haunted locations are the Terry Redlin Art Center, Codington County Heritage Museum, Bramble Park Zoo, Mellette House and the Public Opinion Building Murals.

Goss Opera House

A ghost story from Alice:

> *I heard the Goss building was haunted, so I wanted to see for myself. We drove to Watertown and stood on the sidewalk hoping to pick up on any strange things. I am a bit of a medium myself. I closed my eyes, and I don't know if I was just imagining it or if it really happened, but I started to feel really dizzy. Next thing I know, these weird images were flashing in my mind. I saw a woman screaming. I saw a hallway. I saw flames. I felt a lot of sadness, like around my heart. We decided to call it a night. The next day, I did some research on the building and discovered a woman had been killed there by her son! Stranger yet, he had set her on fire! It really freaked me out.*

One of the more popular haunted places in northeast South Dakota is the Goss Opera House in Watertown. Built by Watertown developer Charles "Fodder" Goss (1833–1905) in 1888, it opened its glorious doors the following year, and it boasted a whopping 1,500 seats for excited theatergoers to sit back in luxury while watching the show. The Goss Opera House was the largest opera house in South Dakota at the time.

Charles Goss was a strong and independent man who brought many opportunities to Watertown. He was born in Newport Pagnell, England. At age eleven, he traveled the long journey to the United States with his parents, making their home in New York for some time. Goss later moved to Sparta, Wisconsin, where he developed many useful skills. For two decades, he worked as a farmer, barber, ice seller, carpenter and more. When he was twenty-one, he moved to Sparta, Wisconsin, where he lived for twenty years, operating a livestock farm. He married Cordelia Hayward (?–1873) in 1856, and they proceeded to have eight children together. Unfortunately, tragedy would consistently strike the Goss family until he had lost his wife and all seven of his sons. His only daughter, Emma, also died young (in 1897, at age twenty-eight) and left her week-old infant in his care. Goss then married Mary Brown and had four children with her.

In 1879, the new Goss family moved to Watertown, South Dakota, and opened a general store. (They hauled the lumber to build it all the way from Wisconsin.) From there, Goss's endeavors blossomed. But he was forced to overcome several more obstacles, as his original building burned down in 1888. The fire cost him thousands of dollars, but Goss never wavered in his faith in both family and business. He immediately started planning his next steps.

In June, he started a foundation that would include sixty-five feet of frontage on Kemp Avenue and twelve feet on Maple. He has his eyes set on building a large public hall, but locals discouraged that idea. Goss planned instead to build a more glorious and bigger opera house than either of the two already standing—one just across the street and another a block away. His building would have seven storerooms on the main level and a grand opera house on the second and third levels. He would offer office space for rent on the main level.

His most glorious undertaking was the fabulous brick Goss building on the corner of Maple Street and Kemp Avenue. The building was revered as one of the most magnificent structures in Watertown and considered a monument to Mr. Goss's enterprise.

The Goss Opera House in Watertown holds a dark story within its beautiful walls. *Courtesy of author.*

In 1892, adventurous Watertown hosted the Mississippi Valley Spiritualism Association for the Forty-Fourth Anniversary of Modern Spiritualism event. This exciting event was held at the Goss Opera House, with Anna Orvis (from Chicago) as the key speaker. She entertained the public with her impressive psychometric readings.

The Merchants' Carnival came to Watertown in 1889, dazzling citizens with glamourous costumes and an exciting show of sixty "banner girls" wearing dresses that represented various local businesses. As the girls danced and paraded around the opera house, everyone was enthralled.

The Goss Opera House amused locals and visitors for many years to come, and Watertown became known as the epicenter for arts and culture.

Charles Goss died suddenly at age seventy-two on January 16, 1906. He will always be remembered as one of the most adventurous and respected original pioneers of Watertown. Who knows, maybe the spirit of Goss himself still roams around his wonderful building.

BUT OTHERS FEEL THE lovely opera house is home to a restless female spirit that loves to linger in its hallways.

Some say the ghost that lingers was once a traveling performer named Annie, awaiting her next curtain call for all eternity. Some speculate Annie's ghost haunts the opera house because she tragically died on the property, but no records have been found to warrant this rumor.

Paranormal investigators suggest that the ghost is that of a former waitress named Maud Alexander who worked at the Lincoln Hotel in Watertown and once rented a room at the Goss. During the Great Depression, many people became broke and homeless. Times were tough, and stress levels were high. As things got worse for locals, the Goss Opera House began renting out rooms on the second and third floors as affordable housing. In March 1936, a tragic family argument quickly turned into a horrific murder. Maud had a son who was a known town drunk, named Orval Alexander. No matter how hard Maud tried to get Orval off the sauce, she never succeeded, and he continued to drink in excess.

On March 13, around eleven o'clock at night, Goss renters heard loud screams coming from apartment no. 6, where forty-eight-year-old Maud lived with her son. Startled, they quickly moved into the hallway to, hopefully, help the woman in distress.

Next, they heard Maud scream out, "Help! I am burning up! I am burning up!" from inside the apartment. Soon, the door of room no. 6 flew open and Maud came running out into the hall with her dress on fire. Onlookers Frank Collier and Nels Pearson acted fast and wrapped the woman in a blanket, trying to quench the flames. A W.E. Wilson ran as fast as he could to Kirman's Confectionary across the street to call for help and summon the police and a doctor. Back at the Goss, Orval just stood by, completely calm and obviously drunk, watching his mother burn.

Help arrived, and Maud was rushed to the nearby Bartron Hospital for treatment of her extensive burns. She had suffered severe burns on three-quarters of her body, and the doctors knew they were unable to save her. Helpless, all they could do was administer medicine to help her with the intense, unbearable pain.

Officials asked Maud what had happened, wanting to record the details of the accident. She claimed on her deathbed that she "accidentally caught fire while trying to light the oil stove," but both the police inspector and the coroner had already looked inside the stove for evidence of a fire and found none. Why would she be lying? And if it was not the stove, then how exactly did Maud catch fire? Everyone wondered…

Poor Maud died in misery the next morning from her burns.

Orval, the only other person in apartment no. 6 at the time of the fire, was immediately taken into custody under suspicion and put in a jail cell to sober up. The next morning, on waking, the hungover Orval broke down and told his unfathomable story to the police. "I started drinking Thursday night and continued all day on Friday," he revealed. "Beer in the morning, and whiskey and sleeping tablets in the evenings." The night of the fire, he said, "I had enjoyed a quick drink with my mom, and then went peacefully off to bed to sleep off the booze." Yet when pressed, he could not remember anything else from the evening in question.

The police broke the news to him that his mother had passed away from her burns.

As the funeral was underway for poor Maud, her son Orval was locked up behind bars and charged with her murder. As he slowly sobered up more, he remembered more details about the night of the fire. As shocked officials gathered around, he confessed the grisly details of his mother's untimely demise.

Later, when Orval stood on the witness stand, he said, "I am guilty of intentionally burning my mother. We were fighting. I poured alcohol on her while she was sleeping on the couch. Then I threw a match on her. After she caught on fire, I just went back into my bedroom and continued my drinking."

Judge Skinner was not impressed with the young man, and the jurors were sickened by his story. Orval was quickly sentenced to thirty years in prison at the South Dakota State Penitentiary. After serving twenty-seven years of his thirty-year sentence, he died in 1963. He is buried in Mt. Hope Cemetery in Watertown—in the same cemetery as the mother he tragically murdered.

Does Maud haunt the Goss Opera House because she is angry at her son for his horrific actions? Or is she still protecting him from beyond the grave? Some people think she refuses to leave room no. 6 because she is still worried about her son, even after what he did to her.

Apparently, a mother's love is eternal.

THE BEAUTIFUL GOSS OPERA House is still standing today at 100 East Kemp Avenue in Watertown (now part of the Mavericks Steakhouse building). Although it fell into disrepair, from 2017 to 2022, $5 million in renovations were completed, with everyone hoping to bring the historic building back to its former glory.

Room no. 6 has been left exactly as it was found before any remodeling began, and the door is kept locked in honor of Maud. Piano music can be heard when no one is playing. Objects are moved around by invisible hands. And the faint odor of smoke can be smelled at times. Who knows, maybe the spirit of Charles Goss himself looms in the hallways and rooms as he wishes to never leave his incredible building!

Enter the Goss Opera House for yourself, and maybe you will experience the apparition of Maud Alexander roaming the halls. If you do not see any ghosts, then pop downstairs and enjoy a delicious steak!

Watertown City Auditorium

The haunted Watertown City Auditorium once housed an old jail. Several witnesses have seen a spectral face floating in the air and lights adjusting by themselves and heard unexplained screams and phantom footsteps in the basement.

No one really knows who—or what—is making the strange phenomena occur in the building. Until the ghost reveals its true identity, the mystery will continue.

Returned from the Grave

In 1910, a Watertown resident was told a true ghost story about a dying woman who threatened to haunt her husband if he ever remarried. In fact, she did return from the dead to scare the daylights out of the man's new wife. She also managed to frighten her ex-husband to death.

Phillip Hartman married a woman named Fanny, who was plain-looking and slightly older than himself. The marriage seemed peculiar to locals, but since Fanny came from a wealthy family, they had their ideas about the reason for Phillip's interest.

But Fanny did not listen to gossip, as she was deeply in love with Phillip. After just two years of marriage, Fanny suffered from some sort of poisoning. She became gravely ill. On her deathbed, she pulled her husband close and whispered, "Phil, I am going to leave you soon. Remember, if you marry again, I swear I will haunt you. I will never let another woman have you! Now kiss me, darling."

With one last kiss, Fanny was gone.

Some time passed, yet Phillip was inconsolable. He could not eat or sleep. It became apparent that Phillip and Fanny truly had been in love. His friends and family tried to reassure Phillip that time would heal his broken heart and he would find true love again.

After about a year, Phillip did take notice of another woman who caught his eye: Amelle Kinkaid. Amelle was everything Fanny was not. She was charming, beautiful and even younger than Phillip—the type of woman Fanny would have been deathly jealous of! Phillip was so smitten with Amelle that he decided to throw caution to the wind and get remarried. The couple was madly in love.

Just a few months after their marriage, Phillip received a handsome job offer that would take the newlyweds to California. They packed their few belongings in Watertown and made the long journey west to start their new life together.

A few weeks later, Phillip came down with a horrible stomachache. He was soon bedridden, and Amelle refused to leave his side for three days. On the fourth day, he seemed to recover enough for Amelle herself to finally take a much-deserved nap. But she did not rest long.

Soon, Amelle came rushing back into Phillip's bedroom, crying hysterically. "Phillip! Phillip!" she yelled. "Fanny is after me! She has come to take you. I have had you long enough, she declares, and now she is going to have you for herself. But I will not give you up, I will not!"

Phillip tried to calm his wife by telling her she was only tired and imagining things. "Calm down, Amelle. This is all nonsense," he told her, hoping she would settle down.

"No, it is not!" she persisted. "I saw her as distinctly as I see you now. I know it is her from her picture. She had on a brown dress, and she is furious. 'He is my husband, not yours,' she told me. 'You have had him long enough,' she said, pointing her finger at me! 'Now I mean to take him as I said I would.' Tell me, Phillip, did she ever say such a thing to you?"

Phillip was in shock. Could his dead wife really return from the grave to carry out her death threat? He decided it was best to lie to his new wife. "No, no. Of course not! Such things are just folly. Here, lie down here on the bed, and I will fetch you a nice glass of wine."

Amelle lay down on the bed and tried to calm her nerves. Perhaps a glass of wine would help, she thought.

Phillip turned and left the room to retrieve the promised glass of wine. No sooner had he gone through the door than Amelle saw her husband pause in the corridor. Next, she heard the sound of gurgling, as if her husband were choking on something. Then she saw him throw up his arms as if warding off an invisible attacker.

Amelle stood frozen in fear as she saw her husband fall to the floor. His final word, just before he died, was, "*Fanny!*"

Did Fanny really keep her promise to haunt her husband if he remarried? Was Fanny capable of somehow killing her husband from the afterlife? Or was it simply fear that caused Phillip to die? How did Amelle know about the threat if she did not hear it from the ghost of Fanny herself, since Phillip never disclosed the deathbed threat about remarrying to her? There are many unanswered questions in this true-life ghost story.

The Seven Mysterious Skulls

In 1913, several students from Watertown High School were off on a picnic at Stoney Point when they made a horrible discovery. The group was hiking in the woods when, suddenly, they spotted a skull sticking out of a steep bank near the water.

Nervous but excited, the students began digging with whatever makeshift tools they could use. Soon, they discovered more bones. Deciding they'd

An unidentified man examines several skulls in his studio in 1926. *Courtesy of LOC, Harris & Ewing photographer, #2016888106.*

better not disturb the bones further, they notified officials, and it was made apparent that the students had been picnicking on an old Native burial site.

The full skeleton was unearthed, and a Dr. Weldon, on inspecting the remains, stated they belonged to a Native American male who was about fifty to sixty years old when he died. He also believed the bones had been buried there for over 100 years!

Did the students dig up more than bones? Some paranormal investigators believe that the disturbance of a burial site can rouse restless spirits and hauntings will soon follow.

Who were these Native Americans? No further information has been discovered about where these historic remains are now. Were they reburied? Are they in a box on a shelf somewhere? It remains an unsolved mystery.

De Smet

The town of De Smet was founded in 1880 with the arrival of the Chicago and Northwestern Railroad, which provided an easier mode of transportation than horses or oxen for people, livestock, supplies and goods. The town was named after Father Pierre-Jean De Smet, a Belgian Jesuit missionary who actively collaborated with Native American tribes in the area. Before the arrival of the railroad, Dakota Sioux Natives primarily inhabited the region. The establishment of the railroad led to the rapid growth and development of the town of De Smet.

One of the most recognized aspects of De Smet's history is its association with the famous author Laura Ingalls Wilder. She and her family lived in De Smet during the late 1880s. Her books, including *By the Shores of Silver Lake*, *The Long Winter*, *Little Town on the Prairie* and *These Happy Golden Years*, provided a detailed look at life in the small town and the hardships the locals faced.

The De Smet Cemetery holds many of the town's early settlers and many Ingalls family members. The cemetery is worth a stroll through. Maybe a ghost or two will pop out from behind a tombstone!

Laura Ingalls Wilder Historic Home

A ghost story from Traci of Montana:

> *I was visiting my friends in South Dakota, and I really wanted to go visit the Ingalls place in De Smet.* Little House on the Prairie *was a fond part of my childhood. I was so excited! As I walked around the grounds, it was so fascinating to me. I tried to visualize things as they were back then, the hardships families had to endure, the troubles they had to overcome. We are so spoiled today! Once I thought I saw a little girl wearing a type of dirty smock sitting on an old, overturned bucket. Her face was a little smeared with dirt. I wondered if this little girl was lost or had wandered from her parents. I turned to tell my girlfriend Sandy that we should go see if the little girl needed help. I no sooner turned my head when the little girl and bucket vanished into thin air! I often wonder to myself who she was and why she chose to reveal her spirit to me.*

A photograph of Laura Ingalls Wilder, author of *Little House on the Prairie*, in 1885. *Courtesy of Wikimedia, public domain, #2511787.*

Thousands of visitors flock to De Smet, South Dakota, every year to enjoy walking on the grounds and touring the historic buildings that once belonged to a much-loved author, Laura Ingalls Wilder. There one can see an exact replica of the original Ingalls home, enjoy covered wagon rides, participate in children's activities, relax while camping and much more. This amazing site features a look at what life was like living on the farm back in the good old days. Kids can even attend class in the First School of De Smet—the very place where Laura and her sister, Carrie, went to school.

But some claim there is more than tourists and employees roaming the grounds. Pa and Ma Ingalls loved their homestead so much that they refuse to leave, even today. Whether the site is truly haunted or not is yet to be discovered, but rumors of cold spots, disembodied voices and shadowy figures have been retold by many.

Perhaps the ghost couple enjoys observing the fun activities at the museum or are simply curious about all the people roaming around—no one knows. Caroline and Charles Ingalls (popularly known as Ma and Pa Ingalls) moved to De Smet in 1879. The following year, Charles selected his homestead spot: a whopping 160 acres of Dakota Territory land free for the taking. All this incredible land only cost Charles and Caroline sixteen dollars in filing fees.

The Ingalls family lived in the surveyor's house until their own home was completed in 1887. Charles worked for the railroad, but the family also worked extremely hard planting gardens, building sheds and digging a well for water. The family was close, and many fond memories were made at the Ingalls home. It is no wonder Ma and Pa's spirits desire to hang around!

Young Laura married Almanzo Wilder in 1885. The couple continued to live happily on the Ingalls homestead for another four years. The rest of the Ingalls family lived on the homestead for another three years after that, until everyone moved into the bigger house that Charles had built.

Married life was hard for Laura. Although Almanzo was a very diligent worker, the couple struggled day to day to make ends meet. Soon their daughter, Rose, was born in 1886. The first four years of marriage provided many complications. Dreadful droughts, large farming debts and more caused much strain in their relationship. In 1888, diphtheria ran rampant. Diphtheria is a highly contagious disease that causes inflammation of the mucous membranes. This bacterial infection, when severe, can also cause difficulty in breathing and swallowing as well as fatal heart and nerve damage. Both Laura and Almanzo contracted the disease. Tragically, Almanzo's legs became paralyzed. Although he partially recovered, weakness made farming too difficult for him. In 1889, the birth and death of their infant son left another deep scar on their hearts.

Hoping for a fresh start, the couple moved to Florida for a year, but they soon returned to De Smet. Yet things continued to get worse. When their home burned down and interest rates soared to a whopping 36 percent, they decided together to give up on the hard life of farming. Almanzo and Laura moved away from South Dakota again in 1890. They were off to Minnesota, where his family had a farm—and the couple and their daughter would finally have some rest from their incredibly stressful past few years.

But their rest period would not last long. The family up and moved to Florida a second time, hoping the mild weather would help Almanzo's bad legs. The weather did help Almanzo, but Laura could not stand the heat and humidity, so they packed their trunks once again and returned to De Smet, South Dakota. Laura, Rose and Almanzo were back home with Ma and Pa Ingalls to enjoy family time together.

Ever restless, in 1894, the Wilder family loaded their covered wagon once more and headed to Mansfield, Missouri (almost seven hundred miles away). They deposited one hundred dollars toward a home and acreage of land, which they called Rocky Ridge Farm. The family enjoyed Rocky Ridge very much. They settled down on the two-hundred-acre farm, which included a small farmhouse, a barn and other outbuildings. The farmhouse served as the Wilders' primary residence. This farm is significant in the life of Laura Ingalls Wilder, as it is where she wrote her beloved series of books.

Laura must have logged all the hardships, developments, family traditions, local issues and other interesting facts of her life during the American West era between 1870 and 1894, for this is what she wrote about in her famous series, *Little House on the Prairie*, later in life. Her first book was published in 1935 (finally accepted after many rejections) and several of Laura's books were published thereafter. (She was finally successful at age sixty-five!). What became a beloved and iconic series of children's books chronicle the adventures and hardships of the Ingalls family as they pioneered their way across the American frontier.

Laura, Almanzo and Rose continued to live on Rocky Ridge Farm in peace and quiet for the rest of their lives.

Almanzo and Laura died in 1949; Rose died in 1957. Today, Rocky Ridge Farm is a popular tourist attraction and museum dedicated to the life and legacy of Laura Ingalls Wilder. Visitors can explore the farmhouse, see the Wilders' belongings and gain insight into the daily life of this pioneering couple.

Could Laura's spirit also be lingering around the historic Ingalls buildings, with Ma and Pa's ghosts, in De Smet, where she made such fond family memories? Possibly!

NOTE: Rocky Ridge Farm is located at 3060 Highway A, Mansfield, Missouri, 65704.

The Bloody Benders

A strange, creepy and little-known story about Laura Ingalls Wilder's childhood life is her family's near-miss encounter with one of the earliest-known serial killers in Kansas. Laura was born on February 7, 1867, in a log cabin near Pepin, Wisconsin. As part of the family's westward expansion in the United States, her family moved to Kansas, then Minnesota, then Iowa and, finally, South Dakota during her childhood and early adulthood.

In 1937, Laura disclosed the disturbing details of how her father would often stop at a farm called Benders that was situated about halfway between their own farm and the small town of Independence, Kansas. The farm of the Bloody Benders was located in Labette County, Kansas, near the town of Cherryvale.

At the Benders', Laura and her Pa would stop to water their horses. Laura remembered Pa would never allow them to go into the store or even get out of the wagon to stretch their legs. They noticed the Benders were always plowing their garden, although oddly, no garden was ever planted.

The Bender Inn and General Store was run by the eerie Bender family between 1871 and 1873. Travelers would often stop at the inn for a good night's rest. Little did they know it would be their last. Many believe the Benders brutally killed over a dozen unsuspecting tourists. They lured travelers into their home on false pretenses and murdered them for their money and possessions. Their motive may have been more than robbery—they may have also enjoyed the thrill they received from murdering people.

1 Grave of Dr. York—2 Grave of McKenzie—3 Grave o' Brown—4 Grave of Longuor and child—5 Hole where Boyd was buried—6 Grave of Jones—7 Grave of McKown—8 Cellar hole—9 House moved from over cellar—10 Little stone stable—11 Sign "This Claim Taken by Wm. Dick—† Little apple trees.

A hand-drawn map of the graves at the farm of the serial killers called the Bloody Benders in 1895. *Courtesy of the* Erie (KA) Record, *May 10, 1895.*

Did Pa know more about the Bloody Benders than he let on?

Later, a man named William York showed up at the Bender Inn looking for his missing brother, Alexander York. This inquiry must have tipped off the Benders that they would soon be investigated, as they left the premises in a hurry. When the police arrived at the inn, they discovered the grisly corpse of a man in the cellar whose skull was bashed in by a blunt object. The shocked police began searching the garden and outbuildings for more bodies, and unfortunately, they found almost a dozen more victims. They even found the remains of a little girl whom they believed was buried alive next to her father.

More victims were discovered slowly. Strangely, a lot of them had lived in Independence, Kansas, where Laura and her family lived. The Bender Inn was situated on the single road that took people from Fort Scott to Independence.

Sheriff Scott and his crew uncovered the bodies buried in the Bender parcel one by one. Some of the known victims were:

- Benjamin Brown from Cedarvale, Kansas, had just purchased a new wagon and team of fine horses when he was traveling through from Osage Mission. He stopped at the Bender Inn for a good night's sleep. It was known he had only about forty dollars on him at the time of his murder.
- Alexander York, a promising Kansas politician, had disappeared earlier.
- W.F. McCrotty was identified by a tattoo on his left arm: "123 Ills. Inf'ty Co. D."
- Mr. John Doe, a small-framed man, was found buried in the well. His body had also been burned. His true identity was never discovered.
- H.F. McKenzie had just left the residence where he had stayed the night six miles from the Benders in November 1872. He was scheduled to visit his sister in Independence when he went missing. McKenzie was a very strong man, who was just twenty-nine years old. Originally from Indiana, he had fought in the Battle of Chickamauga. Locals could not believe anyone could outpower him, but sadly, the Benders did.
- G.W. Langchore (or Lonquor) was traveling with his eight-month-old baby girl when they disappeared. Langchore was taking the girl to her dead mother's family, west of Independence. The poor girl was buried alive in the shallow grave with her father's body.
- John Boyd disappeared while walking the long trek of twenty miles from Independence to Parsons, Kansas, to look for employment. He was never seen again until his body was discovered.
- Dr. William York lived in Independence. He disappeared while traveling to Fort Scott to sell a house. He would soon become a Bender victim.

Top: An illustration of the Bloody Benders' home and how they staged the murders. *Courtesy of the* Erie (KA) Record, *May 10, 1895.*

Bottom: The Bloody Benders—(*left to right*) John Sr., Elvira, John Jr. and Kate—who were some of the earliest known serial killers. *Courtesy of John Towner James, Kan-Okla Publishing Company, Wichita, Kansas, 1913.*

When Pa Ingalls and his friends heard of the horrible deaths at the Benders', they gathered their rifles and decided to join the posse of Sheriff Scott, Colonel York and their team to hunt down the killers. The fugitives were tracked down as they were fleeing toward Chetopa, Kansas, just four miles from the Grand River. Without a moment's hesitation, all four of the Benders—John Sr., Elvira, Kate and John Jr.—were shot on sight and then unceremoniously buried in a mass grave.

It is frightening to think of all the times Laura Ingalls and her family stopped at the Bloody Benders farm to innocently water their horses—and could have become the next victims of the ruthless Bloody Bender family!

NOTE: Laura Ingalls Wilder Historic Homes and Ingalls Homestead is located at 20812 Homestead Road, De Smet, SD 57231.

GARY

Haunted School for the Blind

The beautiful, historic spot in Gary that is now called Buffalo Ridge Resort accommodates weddings, live music and fine dining and features an immaculate hotel and much more. But it is said that the spirit of a small girl haunts the picturesque grounds. Her laughter can be heard now and then when no children are present.

The history of the unique buildings and grounds is quite fascinating. Built in 1872 as the first school for the blind, it provided students a wonderful atmosphere to learn such skills as braille, broom-making and piano tuning alongside their regular academics. It housed nine buildings on its picturesque thirty-seven acres and could accommodate fifty to sixty students. At the school, the students also raised chickens, hogs and dairy cattle and took care of a bountiful vegetable garden.

One of the buildings was the boys' dormitory (now nineteen luxurious hotel rooms). Woodbury Hall (now the Sundance Ballroom) was once the girls' dormitory, complete with an upper stage for the auditorium.

In 1935, the school built underground tunnels for the students to make it easier for them to move from classroom to classroom during the snowy months on campus.

Over the years, the old administration building became Clementine's Bed & Breakfast.

But soon, the old buildings would become vacant and fall into disrepair—a lonely reminder of the past for three long decades.

Then, in 1962, after a tragic accident, Lake Elsie was filled in by the city. Rumors persisted about the old school and lake. Luckily, an adventurous businessman named Joe Kolbach purchased the estate in 2008 with the dream of turning it into a beautiful resort. In 2009, the lake was refilled and restored to its original beauty; it now holds numerous trout.

In 2010, the old Clementine's Bed & Breakfast was restored and turned into the fantastic nineteen-room historic Herrick Hotel with a fine restaurant called the Rock Room Bar & Grill downstairs that features a unique motorcycle theme and can accommodate large parties.

Perhaps stop by or stay at beautiful Buffalo Ridge Resort and see if the little girl ghost shows herself to you! Possibly she was one of the students from so long ago, who refuses to leave the place she once called her home.

NOTE: Buffalo Ridge Resort is located at 1312 Coteau Street in Gary, South Dakota. https://buffaloridgeresort.com.

CHAPTER 2
PARANORMAL HOT SPOTS

*The paranormal is a glimpse into the mysteries
that lie beyond the surface of our everyday lives.*
—Unknown

ANCIENT BURIAL MOUNDS

Scattered throughout South Dakota are ancient burial mounds that still hold the sacred souls of local Native Americans. Hundreds of these mounds have been disturbed due to construction, the bones being revealed along with arrowheads, pottery, tomahawks and hand hammers. While some of the bones have been reburied or moved to a more appropriate location, it is still considered bad luck to disturb the bodies. An old legend says that anyone who digs into an Native burial mound will meet with quick and brutal vengeance.

The lingering souls of the old skeletons could certainly be haunting the mounds. Fort Sisseton has dozens of burial mounds on its grounds—it is one of the largest mound sites in South Dakota. Researchers actively dug up two of the many mounds in order to discover more clues about who these people were. They found eight skeletons in one mound and thirteen in another (the bones were reburied).

More mounds were found near Lake Poinsett (north of Brookings). These may hold the remains of members of the Sisseton Wahpeton tribe and are

Ancient Indian burial mounds are scattered throughout South Dakota. If disturbed, restless spirits might become angry. *Courtesy of LOC #2019701665.*

believed to be five hundred years old. Dozens of mounds can also be found near Sioux Falls, which hold the ancestors of the Sioux tribe.

More burial mounds have been found near Big Stone Lake, Lake Traverse and Hartford Beach. The first White settlers in Big Stone and Lake Traverse arrived after the war of 1812. These men often traded goods and furs with the local Natives. In Big Stone, the mounds hold Sioux known as the Omahas, who possibly came to the area around 1600, but this has not been proven.

The burial mounds are sacred sites that house thousands of souls. Should they be disturbed or left at peace?

Chased by a Ghost

In 1908, a local laborer named Pat was walking late at night to his home on the outskirts of Watertown when he received the shock of his life. As he passed a small cemetery, a ghostly figure stepped out from behind a monument. The man quickly became frightened and started to run. He ran as fast as he could from the ghost, but no matter how fast he ran, the ghost was right behind him. Frightened half to death, he tripped over a big stick and fell to the ground. He felt a sharp pain in his shin and feared he had fractured his leg.

The ghost sat down next to Pat on a log. It proceeded to smile, gave Pat a hearty slap on his shoulder and said, "Say, didn't we go some?"

Pat did not know what to do or say. Finally, he told the ghost, "Yes, and just as soon as I get my breath, we are gonna go some more!"

Pat did catch his breath and resumed his homeward walk, but the ghost finally gave up the chase. Pat could not shake the scary incident from his mind.

Who was the ghost, and why did he choose to follow Pat? Did the ghost just enjoy frightening people, or was he lonely? With so many dead people buried in the cemetery, it would be hard to determine who the ghost might have been.

Or did Pat possibly just let his imagination get away from him?

THE LEGEND OF THE GREY BROTHERS

In November 1958, two Dakota Indian brothers mysteriously died while trapping. Both Clarence (1918–1958) and Joseph (1921–1958) Grey were expert hunters, fishermen and trappers—so why did they meet their untimely demise that fateful evening?

There was a terrible storm the night they died, but the men were surely accustomed to the severe weather. Joseph had fought in World War II and received a Purple Heart for his serious injuries. Both men had excellent survival skills, so many questions arose about their mysterious deaths.

Locals and their families were perplexed about where the brothers had gone and why. They believed they were just exploring and would soon return safe and sound. But the brothers never returned. When the spring thaw came, their decomposed corpses were found. Coroners suspected foul play. The brothers were given a proper burial, but their killer was never found.

It is said that during harsh winters when the wind blows through the tall pine trees, the soft voices of the Grey brothers can be heard singing delightful Dakota Indian melodies.

Why do the spirits of Clarence and Joseph Grey haunt the location where they tragically died? Do their restless souls want the murderer to be discovered?

How come nobody was actively searching for the men between November and April? No follow-up story has been found, and no coroner's reports were filed.

During a stormy night, you can drive down Highway 10, head 0.3 miles east of 451st Avenue in Sisseton and roll your window down and listen. Perhaps you will catch the faint sound of a sad Dakota hymn coming from the Grey brothers out in the distance.

THE GUIDING THORNDSON SISTERS

Tragedy struck the Thorndson family one blizzardy night in 1903. Knut Thorndson, originally from Norway, decided to take his two eldest daughters, Theoline (age thirteen) and Menne (age fifteen) along on a sleigh ride to their neighbor's house. Tobias and Bertha Herigstad (also originally from Norway) were just a quarter of a mile away. His wife, Caroline, decided to stay home with their three youngest children—a decision that may have saved their lives.

As the storm grew worse, Knut decided they'd better leave their neighbors' and head back home as quickly as possible. As the horses tucked their heads down, bracing themselves against the icy, freezing air, the Thorndsons huddled together in the sled, hoping to arrive home sooner than later, safe and sound.

But the Grim Reaper had other plans.

The sled struck a big rock and broke apart. Unable to repair the sled in the stormy conditions, Knut Thorndson decided to unhitch the horses and lead them all back to the safety of their barn and home. He told Theoline and Menne to grab hold of the horses' tails and not let go. The three people and two horses continued on their way toward home in the storm, but the snow was becoming so dense it was hard to see in front of them.

When Knut finally arrived at the barn, exhausted, he turned and noticed something horrible. Both girls were missing.

Frantic, he hurriedly retraced his steps back toward the Herigstads' place. He called and called for the girls until he was hoarse, but there was never an answer. Due to the storm, visibility was practically zero. His

While sleighing in 1893 during a storm, sisters Theoline and Menne Thorndson accidentally froze to death and their ghosts now guide weary travelers to safety. *Courtesy of LOC, F.M. Lamb., photographer, 1894, #99401488.*

search continued, but the young girls were never found. The freezing storm continued late into the night.

The next morning, the search for the girls continued, even though the worst was feared.

Tragically, about four hundred yards from the Herigstads' farm, the two girls were found huddled together, frozen to death. Knut Thorndson never stopped blaming himself for the deaths of his two daughters.

It is said that the girls' spirits have taken a shine to helping others in need during winter storms, gently and invisibly steering them in the direction of the old Herigstad farm for protection. Over the past century, several travelers have told stories of somehow being rescued from the harsh winter storms typical of the Coteau des Prairies. They speak of being mysteriously led to safety by an unknown force that guides them to the hospitality of the Herigstad family homestead.

Can the spirits of the Thorndson girls really guide weary travelers to safety? Stranger things have been known to happen.

NORTHERN STATE UNIVERSITY

For fifty years, Jerde Hall at Northern State University in Aberdeen housed college students. Before Jerde Hall was demolished in 2018, it was haunted by the ghost of a little girl. Students residing on the fourth floor repeatedly saw the ghost of a small girl running up and down the hallways. Sometimes her ghost would stand at the end of student's beds, whisper, "Shh…" and giggle. Other people saw her cute image reflected in a mirror. Who was this little girl? Why did she feel the need to roam the dormitory?

The Jerde Hall building was replaced by the South Dakota School for the Blind and Visually Impaired. No reports have been recorded by the staff of any more appearances by the little ghost girl. Did she disappear along with the old building? The little girl's identity is a mystery to this day.

A SECOND BUILDING AT Northern State University that is reportedly haunted is the Johnson Fine Arts Center on campus. It was built in the 1970s. The ghost of a male entity has been seen walking the halls, sometimes whistling. He enjoys playing with the lights, turning them on and off for no reason. He also likes to move objects. Others have reported the sound of keys jingling, like the sets of keys a janitor typically carries. Perhaps the ghost once worked for the school and refuses to leave?

Entry columns and campus quadrangle at Northern State University in Aberdeen. The campus reportedly has two ghosts. *Courtesy of LOC, Carol M. Highsmith, photographer, #2021756305.*

SOUTH DAKOTA STATE UNIVERSITY

Northern State University is not the only college campus in South Dakota that is haunted. The Doner Auditorium at South Dakota State University in Brookings has its own ghost. A mischievous male spirit entertains himself in Doner Auditorium by playing the organ and messing with the lights. Many witnesses have heard organ music when no one was sitting on the bench. The sweet sound would play at random times.

Some believe the entity is that of a janitor who fell to his death from the alcove above in 1919. Current students have named the ghost George and claim he has his own secret room hidden behind the staircase.

DANCING LIGHTS IN THE SKY

The small, quiet town of Miller, South Dakota, is nestled southwest of Watertown. With a population under two thousand, everyone knows everyone. Founded by Henry Miller, it opened its post office in 1881.

In 1906, a single farmer woman made quite an impression when she fought single-handedly for her land claim. Miss Mattie Gordon, without the support of a spouse, plowed and farmed fifty acres of flax and thirty acres of barley. Eventually, she even became a champion flax farmer!

But her land would soon become known for more than flax—something spectacular and very mysterious. The sight of a cluster of "dancing lights" over her fields every night became a local unexplained mystery. Just west of her home, the flashing and moving lights would hover over her land for hours, perplexing to everyone who saw them.

Since electricity on rural farms in South Dakota was not popular until 1935, where were the lights coming from? What was causing these strange dancing lights, and why were they hanging around Miss Gordon's land? Were they spirit orbs? There was a small cemetery just northeast of her home; was there some sort of paranormal situation that combined the cemetery with her acreage? Who is buried at the cemetery? Could it be the spirit of a former landowner of the Gordon farm or something else? Mysterious dancing lights and orbs have been known to hover over the sites of crop circles prior to their creation. Were these lights somehow increasing Mattie's flax crops with magical energy?

The mystery of the Gordon Lights was never solved.

An unidentified woman working her land. In 1906, Mattie Gordon saw mysterious flashing lights hovering over her fields at night in Miller. *Courtesy of LOC, John Vachon, photographer, 1940, #2017810443.*

SITTING BULL'S DEATH SITES

On the very left edge of our northeast South Dakota boundary is a famous haunted site that is too good to leave out of this book. Stories conflict, but some believe the very spot where the legendary Native American Chief Sitting Bull, also known as Tatanka Iyotake (1831–1890) was killed on the bank of the Grand River is haunted by his spirit.

Others claim his original grave site at Fort Yates, North Dakota, still harbors his restless soul trapped in an army-made coffin. Fort Yates at the time was the tribal headquarters of the Standing Rock Sioux Tribe. Now, a dirt road leads to the marked grave site that is covered by a thick protective slab of concrete for safekeeping. Others are sure that Sitting Bull's final resting place in Mobridge, South Dakota, houses his restless spirit. Still more rumors argue that the moving of Sitting Bull's bones was nothing more than a publicity stunt. No one will ever know the truth, but the story is a good one.

Sitting Bull was one of the greatest leaders of the Hunkpapa tribe. His birth name was Jumping Badger, but while young, he acquired his new name, Sitting Bull. Part of the Lakota Sioux, he killed his first buffalo at age ten. Supposedly, Sitting Bull was also a prophet, and in 1876, he fell into a trancelike state and saw that his people would win a great victory over the White Man. (This would be the Battle at Little Big Horn on June 25, 1876, also known as Custer's Last Stand.)

After many victories and heroic acts, Sitting Bull had developed quite a reputation as a fierce warrior and strong leader. Later in life, he even became part of Buffalo Bill's Wild West show. Yet his victories would come to an end during a horrific clash between Sitting Bull's family and friends and an angry Indian agent named James McLaughlin. McLaughlin held a grudge and ordered the arrest of Sitting Bull. He feared Sitting Bull was going to flee the reservation that his tribe was forced to live on.

But why was Sitting Bull a target? Why did some people want him dead?

In the late nineteenth century, a religious movement called the Ghost Dance emerged among various Native American tribes. The Ghost Dance movement promised the Natives the return of the buffalo, the disappearance of the White settlers and the restoration of Native American lands and their ways of life. Sitting Bull was involved with this movement, and he was viewed as a main figure by some of its followers.

The United States government was threatened by the Ghost Dance movement, believing it could incite resistance and more anger among Native American tribes and represent a potential threat to their authority

Left: Sitting Bull was murdered in 1890 by agents, along with his son Crow Foot and fourteen other men. His bones were stolen and moved to Mobridge, where he was born. *Courtesy of LOC, D.F. Barry, photographer, 1885, #94506170.*

Right: Amos Little, a Sioux American Indian and member of Buffalo Bill's Wild West Show, posed for his portrait in 1900. *Courtesy of LOC, Gertrude Käsebier, photographer, #2006679589.*

and control over tribal lands. Orders were given to arrest Sitting Bull—at any cost.

On December 15, in Dakota Territory on the Grand River, several Indian agents moved in to arrest the great Native American leader. After they announced themselves as agents, Sitting Bull casually got dressed, prepared to calmly talk and work things out with them. But while he was dressing, his son Crow Foot (1873–1890) came to him and said, "You always called yourself a brave chief. Now you are allowing yourself to be taken by the *caska maza* (police)." These words changed Sitting Bull's mind. Now he did not want to back down or cooperate.

Soon his family became agitated at the display of hostility toward Sitting Bull from the agents, and shots were fired at the agents by Catch the Bear. This turned into a deadly frenzy of shouting and more shooting, and many people died as a result.

Without time to flee, Sitting Bull was grabbed and shot in the head and chest. He was killed instantly. Terrified by his father's murder, his young son

Crow Foot, Sitting Bull's son, was murdered by agents the same day as his father. He was only seventeen years old. *Courtesy of LOC, David Francis Barry, photographer, #97500349.*

Crow Foot grabbed a weapon and prepared to fight the police. When the police approached Crow Foot, they grabbed him. He cried out, "I want to live! You have killed my father! Let me go!"

The police did not care. They shot Crow Foot to death as well.

After the bloody massacre, the bodies were piled into one of Sitting Bull's cabins. A week later, the Reverend T.L. Riggs arrived at the cabin to organize a burial. Crow Foot was buried in a mass grave, along with the others who were shot, just outside of Sitting Bull's cabin. Crow Foot was just seventeen years old when he was murdered.

Sitting Bull's body was unceremoniously buried at the United States Army post cemetery at the Standing Rock Reservation at Fort Yates, North Dakota, where his bones spent the next sixty years. Some claim his spirit is still resting there, where his bones have been since 1890.

But Sitting Bull's family was not happy with this situation. The family secured a letter from the Bureau of Indian Affairs stating that Sitting Bull's descendants (not the government) should have the right to pick where his body was buried—and they wanted that to be at Mobridge. The officials at Fort Yates disagreed. Legend states that on April 8, 1953, his descendants (his brother-in-law in particular, Clarence Grey Eagle) and several friends secretly exhumed the body from Fort Yates in the middle of the night and hauled the bones fifty miles away to Mobridge, South Dakota, where Sitting Bull was born. (In 1953, Sitting Bull's grave at Fort Yates was marked with only a simple wooden headstone, not a concrete slab.)

The officers at Fort Yates laughed and told the family that they came too late, as Sitting Bull's body had already been dug up by someone else and moved to Turtle Mountain. They claimed that the bones the family stole were those of a horse or some other person.

Then their story changed again. They claimed that Sitting Bull's body had been buried deep down in quicklime to hasten his decomposition and there was no way they could have stolen his bones. But there must have been something going on, because soon, a concrete slab, bollards and a huge rock were installed—just to make sure no grave robbers could cause havoc at Sitting Bull's final resting place again.

Which story is true? Why would the men at Fort Yates go to all that trouble if Sitting Bull's body was not really there? Or was it simply a way for them not to admit that the exhumation had happened?

Back at Mobridge, the stolen bones were encased in a steel vault that was embedded in a twenty-ton block of concrete, so there would never be a chance again of anyone digging up Sitting Bull's bones. His eternal resting place was high on a bluff proudly overlooking the Missouri River.

To memorialize the site, famous carver Korczak Ziolkowski (who created the Crazy Horse Memorial) was commissioned to carve a seven-ton rock bust in the likeness of the great leader.

No one truly knows where Sitting Bull's remains are buried. Some claim Sitting Bull is restless because of the multiple disputes over his bones and their being buried by the wrong people. Maybe Sitting Bull is simply happy to be loved so much by his family and that they went to such great lengths to bring him home.

The following is a list of the killed and wounded from the fight:
- Sitting Bull, killed, fifty-nine years of age
- Crow Foot (Sitting Bull's son), killed, just seventeen years of age.
- Henry Bull Head, first lieutenant of police, died eighty-two hours after the fight
- Charles Shave Head, first sergeant of police, died twenty-five hours after the fight
- James Little Eagle, fourth sergeant of police, killed in the fight
- Paul Afraid-of-Soldiers, private of police, killed in the fight
- John Armstrong, special police, killed in the fight
- David Hawkman, special police, killed in the fight
- Alexander Middle, private of police, wounded, recovered
- Black Bird, killed, forty-three years of age
- Catch the Bear, killed, forty-four years of age
- Spotted Horn Bull, killed, fifty-six years of age
- Brave Thunder No. 1, killed, forty-six years of age
- Little Assiniboine, killed, forty-four years of age
- Chase Wounded, killed, twenty-four years of age
- Bull Ghost, wounded, entirely recovered
- Brave Thunder No. 2, wounded, but recovered rapidly
- Strike the Kettle, wounded, forced to go to Fort Sully as a prisoner

Notes: The Mobridge grave site is on a bluff across the Missouri River from the town. From US Highway 12, just west of the river, turn south onto Highway 1806 and drive about four miles to the grave.

Directions to the Fort Yates grave site: From Highway 12 in South Dakota, turn onto SD–1806 N (entering North Dakota), continue onto State Highway 1806 N (9.2 miles), turn right onto ND–1806/State Highway 1806 N (2.4 miles), turn right onto 92nd Street (1.8 miles), then turn left onto Dike Road. Your destination will be on the left.

A scan of the fascinating handwritten report (no. 39602) of these events as told by Indian Agent James McLaughlin (although he was not an actual eyewitness of the event) submitted by the Office of Indian Affairs on December 16, 1890, can be read online at: http://www.primeau.org/sittingbull/mclaughlinsreportondec1890.html.

The sworn statement of Wakhutemani or Shoots-Walking (one of the policemen who took part in the affair) can be read at: https://thefirstscout. blogspot.com/2015/12/bullhead-and-last-days-of-sitting-bull.html.

TEKAKWITHA ORPHANAGE SITE

The Sisseton Wahpeton Oyate Community Memorial Park location was once the site of the Tekakwitha Orphanage. The orphanage was home for countless Native American babies up until around the 1970s. The ghost of a little boy has been heard begging to come home with people because he does not want to stay there. The building was demolished around 2010 in order to make way for the park.

Between 1940s and the 1950s, Father John Polen ran the orphanage, and it was called the Tekakwitha Indian Mission—but it has a more sinister

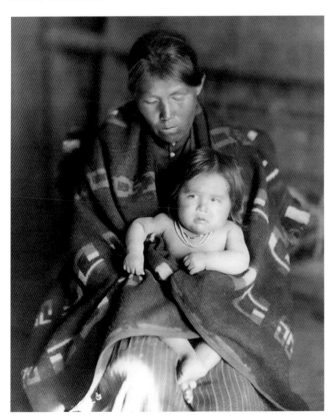

An unidentified Indian woman poses with her baby. Indian children were ruthlessly taken from their mothers on the Lake Traverse Reservation in Sisseton and sold for ten dollars. *Courtesy of LOC, Pennington & Rowland, #2006690075.*

past. History suggests that Native American children were forcibly taken from their mothers, Dakota Sioux women on the Lake Traverse Reservation in Sisseton, and submitted into the mission, where they would be sold or rented out. The going rate for an Native American baby was between ten and fifteen dollars. Many of these children would be "adopted" by families, not to become part of a loving home but to be used as child labor. Sadly, even more sinister stories surfaced about Father Polen and the nuns sexually abusing the children. Although lawsuits were filed and charges brought by those affected, most were dropped or dismissed.

Paranormal investigators have recorded evidence of paranormal activity on the site. Even though the old orphanage has been destroyed, does the land somehow retain negative energy, causing paranormal events to occur?

A BLOODY DEATH SCENE FROM BEYOND

In 1914, a Sisseton man named F.A. Mitchel disclosed that he felt he had been visited by deceased persons and could read minds and even receive messages from the other side.

As a boy, he would constantly think the same things as the person sitting next to him. Coincidence? Mitchel felt he possessed some sort of "wireless" process whereby he could interpret impressions and thoughts. He became so fascinated with the human body and brain that he became a doctor. Later, at the height of his profession, he became incredibly stressed and decided he needed a few days off. A trip to the country would be just what the doctor (himself!) ordered.

Dr. Mitchel stopped at a boardinghouse and decided to stay and rest for a spell. In the evening, he would sit on the porch alone and watch the sun set. He really enjoyed looking at a nearby house that was built sometime during the colonial period. The home had grand pillars on the porch, and Mitchel thought it was the most handsome home in the area.

One night, as he was retiring to bed, he heard what sounded like wagon wheels crunching on the gravel outside. Then came a frantic, loud cry: "Doctor? Are you a doctor?!"

Mitchel opened the window and stuck his head out into the nighttime air. "What's the matter?" he asked.

The man outside seemed flustered and unable to explain the problem to the doctor. "Quick, come with me!" he begged.

The doctor quickly changed from his nightdress into trousers, went downstairs and climbed into the wagon with the stranger. Without even knowing where they were going or why, the doctor tried to get some sort of sense of the nature of the crisis. The stranger offered none.

Soon, they were pulling up to the very house that the doctor had often admired from afar. The men walked up the porch together, surrounded by the strong, tall pillars. After they entered, the doctor said, "This is the very house I have so often admired and dreamt of."

Then Mitchel noticed a young woman, daintily dressed, who appeared to be under a great amount of duress. "Come with me," is all the woman said. He quickly followed the woman up the grand staircase, and they stopped in front of one of the bedroom doors. The woman slowly turned the glass doorknob.

Inside, a frail woman was lying in a four-poster bed with a man holding her hand. On the other side of the bed was a young girl, also holding the patient's hand. When the doctor pulled down the bedsheet to examine the woman, he noticed she was covered in a lot of blood. He could tell the bandages were hastily done and already soaked deep red with fresh blood. Knowing the situation did not look good, he offered to clean her up and rebandage her in a more professional manner.

The injured woman began gasping for air, and the doctor knew it would not be long before she would slip over to the other side.

Strangely, she asked the man next to her, "Are you convinced of the unjustness of your suspicions?"

"Yes, yes. Forgive me," he answered.

"I forgive you. Goodbye."

And with those four parting words, the woman was gone.

The doctor gathered his bag and, with a nod, left the room for the family to grieve alone.

Downstairs, he noticed the people gathered there were wearing clothes from the earlier colonial period. He wondered, *Why are they wearing these costumes?* He recognized their strange neck collars from pictures he had seen of the clothing worn by early settlers.

The same man that picked him up in the carriage loaded the doctor back in and slowly guided the horses back to his home. They rode in silence, the only sounds being the horse occasionally snorting and the crunching of the wagon's wheels. Once home, the exhausted doctor undressed and crawled into bed. He was quickly off to sleep.

The next morning, unable to shake the strangeness of the evening, the doctor asked the others in the boarding house if they had heard the horse-drawn carriage or the man's frantic hollering. None of them had heard a thing.

The doctor began asking around about who was the peculiar family that was currently living in the beautiful colonial down the road from him. To his surprise, he learned that the home had been vacant for over thirty years! On further investigation, he also learned that prior to the Revolutionary War (1775–83), a prominent family had lived in the home, and a horrific crime had been committed there. The woman's husband, maddened by jealousy, viciously murdered his wife by stabbing her to death. Somehow, the doctor had relived this nightmare and watched the scene of the woman dying as clearly as if it were happening right before his eyes!

The strange questions that emerge from this very credible witness of the paranormal activity he experienced that night are many.

- How did the doctor physically see the woman's last moments?
- Why was he (out of the many people who were also in the boardinghouse) selected to view and experience the grisly scene?
- How was the doctor able to actually hear the happenings of the death scene and the conversations between the ghosts?
- How was he actually transported in the middle of the night (in the phantom horse-drawn carriage with the ghost driver) from his home to the mysterious colonial? Or did he somehow sleepwalk all the way there? If so, wouldn't he have woken up somewhere along the way?
- How was he able to feel the bloody blankets and bandages that were wrapped around the poor woman or change a ghost's bandages himself? Or was it simply a dream?
- Although the doctor was interested in developments between electrical currents and the human body, that would not necessarily prime him for paranormal activity. So how and why did it happen?

The experience made such an impression on the doctor that he risked his career and reputation by publicly admitting to and retelling his strange story for all the world to read.

Did the dying woman want the good doctor to tell her story so her husband's horrible deed would not go unpunished? Did she wish her husband to be known as a killer? Why was the doctor summoned thirty years after the murder to witness and retell her story? Was he selected because he was a credible witness and, therefore, the people would be more likely to believe him? If Dr. Mitchel had experienced psychic activity his whole life, then he might have been more prone to receiving messages and visions from the afterlife.

There are many types of paranormal and psychic abilities. To name a few:

- Clairvoyance: psychic seeing of images and flashes of scenes
- Clairaudience: psychic hearing of sounds, voices and communications
- Clairsentience: intuitive feeling and sensing of things both seen and unseen
- Claircognizance: inner knowing of various ideas and facts
- Clairempathy: sensing and/or absorbing the emotions of others
- Telepathy: mind-to-mind communication between subjects
- Psychokinesis or telekinesis: manipulating and moving objects using only the mind
- Psychometry or psychoscopy: obtaining information touching items that hold a person's energy
- Remote viewing, remote sensing or telaesthesia: seeing a distant or unseen target; viewing a scene, building or landmark
- Precognition: perceiving and foretelling future events
- Mediumship or channeling: communicating with spirits or the dead
- Energy healing: transmitting healing energy to others through Reiki, crystals, stones or other forms of energy

So why would a doctor who was not actively or currently involved in the paranormal world, had a good reputation, was considered an upstanding citizen and was not actively pursuing the occult be selected by the spirits in the colonial house to experience the crime?

The mystery will never be solved. Since there are very few clues and little information to go on, it is impossible to research who the woman and her jealous husband were. The colonial house has probably long been demolished, the tragedy becoming just a distant memory.

Many psychic detectives today claim they can "see" crimes as they were being committed and can offer valuable clues and advice to investigators hoping to solve the cases.

A TRAIN WRECK AND GHOSTS

In 1940, the horrific scene of a train wreck left locals saddened. On August 28, the Chicago, Milwaukee, St. Paul & Pacific Railroad train was barreling down the tracks on a run from Aberdeen, South Dakota, to Minneapolis, Minnesota. As the passenger train carrying over fifty people (and three young transients who had also hopped aboard in the hopes of a free ride) traveled past Milbank and onward to Marvin, the unthinkable happened. An unexpected derailment occurred, hurling several of the cars off the tracks and into nearby ditches.

As the train derailed, eight of the passengers were severely injured. Two others were not so lucky. Two of the transients, Roscoe Lecount (age twenty) and Dane Miller (age nineteen), were crushed between the locomotive and the baggage car. Both died instantly on impact. The third transient was injured but not killed.

Engineer Fred Pedlar was also injured when he became wedged between the baggage car and the locomotive. For over two hours, men tried desperately to free Pedlar from his fate. A torch was finally brought in, and slowly, they were able to extract Pedlar from the cars. But his right arm was severely

In 1940, a derailed train like the one pictured killed two teenagers. Roscoe Lecount and Dane Miller were crushed between the locomotive and the baggage car. *Courtesy of LOC, Andrew Russell, photographer, #2005696869.*

Several unidentified people and crew pose in front of a Chicago, Milwaukee & St. Paul train, no. 3027, that stopped in Milbank during the 1890s. *Courtesy of Grant County Historical Society (GCHS).*

mangled. He was quickly taken to the nearby town of Webster, where doctors fought to save his arm. Unfortunately, the surgery was unsuccessful, and the procedure was switched over to an amputation.

When Pedlar was questioned about why he took the curve at such an accelerated rate, he said, "I had just received an urgent telegraph and was eager to get back home as quickly as possible to deal with the situation." Unfortunately, Pedlar's anxiety about the telegram had left two young men dead.

Some say they have seen the ghostly spirits of two teenage hoboes walking along the tracks where the Chicago, Milwaukee, St. Paul & Pacific Railroad once rolled. Perhaps Lecount and Miller are still trying to reach their desired final destination—which certainly was not the site of the derailment.

Why do spirits choose to hang around the sites of their deaths? Are they trapped somehow on Earth, or do they actively choose to stick around? Many ghosts from accidents, suicides and murders continue to haunt us; what is the deciding factor for this? It is a mystery that will perhaps never be solved.

Whiskey and Strychnine: A Deadly Mix

Milbank farmer James Reed (age seventy-one) met his unusual fate one night while partaking in a friendly glass of whiskey. Some say his angry spirit still seeks revenge for his murder and refuses to leave. The Reed ranch was located about three miles northwest of Milbank. Does the restless spirit of Mr. Reed still roam the streets of Milbank searching for his killer? Some claim to have seen the ghostly apparition of a man wearing overalls wandering Main Street late at night.

In 1910, having a telephone in your home was a luxury. Not all farms and residences in town could afford such a lavish frill. A typical party line included six or seven families using a single phone line. Back then, to reach the operator, you had to crank the little handle on the side of the phone box. The operator would answer the signal and ask whom you wished to reach, then she would ring them. The infantile phone system was not always dependable. This was the case when Jessie Reed, James's live-in daughter, was desperate to secure help for her father.

A neighbor, Mrs. Lowthian, heard Jessie's cries for help when she picked up the party line.

"Come quick! Come quick! Papa is sick!" yelled the frightened Jessie.

An unidentified woman posed with a telephone in 1915. Party phone systems were unreliable but still considered a luxury during that era. *Courtesy of LOC, #97510172.*

Not wanting to waste any time, Jessie ran to the nearby Kockx farm. There she encountered Frank Kockx and his brother John, and she quickly explained the situation. They all piled into the Kockx automobile to drive over to the Reed farm.

Ranchers Phil and W.I. Lowthain were also eager to help. They tried to reach a doctor on the Lowthain landline, but the telephones again were not cooperating. They caught wind that Dr. Ferguson was visiting a patient on the Sutcliffe ranch nearby. They drove to meet the doctor over at the Sutcliffes' and begged him to come to the Reed farm with them.

Back at the Reed farm, poor James was succumbing quickly to his ailment. As Dr. Ferguson administered a dose of morphine to calm James down, he asked

James what had happened to him. James was prepared to tell his side of the story on his deathbed. "I have been poisoned by whiskey given to me by John Van Asch!" he replied. Knowing his demise was near, he began giving orders for the division of his property and personal possessions. A few hours later, James Reed was dead.

Reed's corpse was taken to Emanuel and Evans Undertaking in Milbank. An inquest was organized. A warrant for Asch's arrest was signed by W.I. Lowthian and served by Sheriff Cross. When Cross arrived at Asch's farm, Asch stated he had not seen Reed in over a week. He was thrown in jail anyway.

The inquest was to be held at Emanuels and Evans. Several men were rounded up to testify. One man, I.O. Foster, had some curious news about Asch. Foster had been visiting Milbank on Saturday afternoon, wishing to look at old Meyer's property, which was up for sale, He stopped at the Martens Brothers Real Estate office in Milbank to inquire about the property. There he was introduced to agent John Van Asch. When Foster asked Asch to go to the Meyer farm with him, Asch replied hastily, "I will not go within one mile of the Meyer farm!" No explanation for his bizarre outburst was given.

The next man to be questioned about Reed's murder was Henry Cunningham. He disclosed that he had gone to the Reed farm that Friday evening and seen that Reed was in a terrible state of health and suffering from convulsions. Why didn't Cunningham call for a doctor? It seems odd that someone would see a man suffering from convulsions and not call for a doctor. No explanation for this peculiarity was offered.

Reed was a well-liked man in Milbank. It was said he was kind and generous. Even during his personal time of need, not only was Reed praying for his own salvation, but he was also praying for salvation for Asch's murderous soul.

It was soon discovered that Asch owed Reed thirty-two dollars. Was a debt of a mere thirty-two dollars enough to kill a man?

Reed's convulsing lessened as the morphine relaxed his muscles. Again, Reed whispered, "John Van Asch poisoned me!"

Neighbor C.S. Amsden felt compelled to search the Reed farm for evidence. He soon found an empty whiskey bottle that had been tossed on the side of the road. When officials reviewed Asch's purchases in Milbank, it was discovered that the empty bottle found in the ditch was the same size and brand that Asch had bought earlier in town at Ed Johnson's Saloon. To make matters worse for Asch's plea of not guilty, the proprietor at the

A postcard of several unidentified Whetstone Valley Landseekers in front of the beautiful Hotel St. Hubert in Milbank. *Courtesy of GCHS.*

Two unidentified girls in the drugstore on Main Street in Milbank during the 1920s. *Courtesy of GCHS.*

N.J. Bleser Drug Store remembered Asch purchasing strychnine, claiming he "wished to kill some rats in his barn."

On his deathbed, Reed said that Asch had offered him a drink of whiskey, which Reed refused. "He pestered me until I gave in," Reed remembered. He had promised his family he would not drink whiskey anymore. Reed told the officers that Asch also offered young Jessie a drink, but she refused to partake. When Asch asked Reed again to have a drink with him, Reed claimed he had been drinking beer earlier that day and did not want to mix the two. But Asch was relentless and refused to take no for an answer. Reed reluctantly took a swallow of the liquor and immediately noticed the whiskey tasted extremely bitter. He knew he had just been poisoned.

Reed passed away after telling his story to the police, eager to have his murderer captured and punished. His interment was held at Emanuel's with his loved ones present. Reverend Oldfield provided the funeral services. Reed was buried at the Milbank Cemetery.

James Reed was an old soldier who proudly served in the Eleventh Minnesota Volunteer Infantry during the Civil War. He had lived in Grant County for over thirty years and was well-respected by all who knew him.

Asch (age fifty), who had been living in town only twelve years, had a reputation for having a bad temper. In 1902, he had assaulted a local, Frank Order, with a pipe and received a $300 fine and a short sentence in jail.

After his trial for the murder of James Reed, Asch was held in jail in Milbank. No one came to visit him. His wife, Catherine, and his children refused to give him any comfort. He was becoming a problem at the jail, too. He had tried to assault Sheriff Jennings and Officer Derrick, first making a fake body out of bedclothes buried under the blanket so when the officers came to check on the prisoner, they found him in the corner with an iron bar ready to assault them. The men quickly pulled their revolvers and pointed them at Asch.

But justice was served one night when Asch decided to commit suicide and relieve the taxpayers of his burden. On August 11, 1910, Asch tore his county blanket into strips and hanged himself with them.

Did Asch really kill Reed over a few bucks? Was his attempt to kill Jessie planned so there would be no one left alive to tell the story? Was there more to the story than what was told by Reed on his deathbed? This is a classic tale of murder and revenge and the perfect setup for a vengeful ghost.

CHAPTER 3
LAKES AND LEGENDS

Beneath the serene surface of lakes, ancient mysteries
and monstrous secrets may lie hidden.
—Unknown

South Dakota has many lakes strung throughout the glacial region. These were formed during the last huge glacier (during the Wisconsin period between ten thousand and seventy-five thousand years ago). Stories of lost loves, violence, murders and more circle around these beautiful waters.

South Dakota has well over one thousand lakes in the state, and several are involved in local legends and lore that have been passed down for decades.

THE *MUSKEGON* DISASTER

Big Stone Lake covers an area of approximately 12,610 acres and stretches for twenty-six miles from its border between western Minnesota and northeastern South Dakota. The lake has a maximum depth of around sixteen feet. It offers excellent fishing and recreational activities. In the 1757 edition of the Mitchell Map, the lake is shown as "L. Tinton," referring to

The *Muskegon* is now dry-docked in Ortonville, Minnesota, just a few miles from where it capsized, killing seven people, in 1917. *Courtesy of author.*

the Lakota people, also known as Tetonwan ("dwellers of the prairie"). But the beautiful lake also holds a few dark, watery secrets...

On July 10, 1917, the day started out just like every other for Captain Peter Luff. He charged a small fee to haul people and goods back and forth on Big Stone Lake. He proudly ran the paddlewheel steamboat called the *Muskegon*. His boat was termed the grandest ever to run on the lake by locals. It was sixty feet long and extremely luxurious for the era. The upholstery was the finest around, and inside the cabin, polished mahogany impressed the passengers. The boat was built by a Minneapolis millionaire named Tom Shevlin. It was commonly docked at Hartford Beach, South Dakota, while not in use.

On the tenth, Luff was completing his second run for the day. On this trip, he had nine passengers onboard, who were cherishing the leisurely trip to the towns of Big Stone, South Dakota, and Ortonville, Minnesota. The lake was flat and calm.

But just a few miles from their final destinations, the weather took a turn for the worse. A strange, swirling black ball shape came into view high in the sky. Suddenly, everyone on board was scared for their lives. The ginormous, menacing black "ball" soon headed right toward their boat. Within seconds, the water was somehow being sucked high up into the air, and huge waves began pounding against the boat. Terrified, passengers prayed, as Captain Luff tried desperately to keep control of his beloved boat.

An eleven-year-old passenger named David Mengelt clung to whatever he could, trying not be swept away by the raging wind and tossed into the icy water. Isabelle Larson and her two nieces Bessie and Hazel Erickson huddled together, scared to death.

Soon, the waves and wind proved to be more than Captain Luff and the *Muskegon* could manage. The captain tried to direct his boat to the nearest shore in the hopes of keeping his passengers safe. But after one more treacherous wave, the *Muskegon* succumbed and began to capsize.

Passengers Tranberg and the boy Mengelt were trapped inside the cabin as it started to sink. Captain Luff and passenger Albert Nelson were tossed overboard. Nelson tried to hang on to the boat, but soon, he slipped out of sight and sank to the bottom of the lake. The *Muskegon* slowly sank into the icy water, taking all but two people down with it.

The next day, rescuers searched for the bodies, and the *Muskegon* was hauled to shore. The rescuers would not stop until all the victims were found. They succeeded in locating the seven dead: Albert Nelson, Patrick Weatherly, Isabelle Larson and her nieces Bessie and Hazel, Barney Sweeney and Captain Luff. Captain Luff still had a handful of silver dollars in his pocket—the fares he received to transport his passengers safely across the lake.

Some claim to still see strange, dark, swirling clouds in the sky over Big Stone Lake where the tragedy occurred. Others say they can see Captain Luff standing by the water's edge, forever mourning the disaster and the lives that were lost at his command. This is truly a sad tale of a captain going down with his ship.

NOTE: The *Muskegon* has been lovingly cared for and is now dry-docked in Ortonville, Minnesota, just a few miles from where it met its fate in 1917. It can be seen at the Big Stone County Museum along with many artifacts and collectibles. The Big Stone County Museum is located at 985 US Highway 12, Ortonville, Minnesota 56278. Telephone: (320) 839-3359.

ENEMY SWIM LAKE

During 1812, the Sioux (also known as the Santee Dakota) and Chippewa tribes were bitter enemies. One evening, the Sioux tribe was sleeping peacefully by the lake, northeast of Waubay, but the Chippewas had plans

The Chippewas rowed their canoes out into Enemy Swim Lake and slaughtered the members of the Sioux tribe who were sleeping on the shore. *Courtesy of LOC, #99614365.*

to attack and kill them. The Chippewas noticed campfires along the lake, so they loaded into their canoes and began quietly rowing across the lake toward their sleeping rivals.

The Chippewas quickly jumped out of their canoes and into the water, eager for a fight. One of the Sioux woke up and saw the Chippewas coming toward them at Shepherds Point. He frantically called out, "*Toka nuapi! Toka nuapi!*"—"The enemy swims!"

The Chippewas started a bloody battle, and many lost their lives. The Chippewas did not stop until all the Sioux were killed. The lake thus earned its nickname, Enemy Swim Lake. It is located one and a half miles northeast of Waubay Bible Camp. Today, the area is part of the Lake Traverse Indian Reservation.

In 1918, Jack Rommel opened up the Enemy Swim Hotel (also called Camp Dacotah), which could easily accommodate sixty people. Rommel used old Native artifacts he had gathered over the years to decorate his hotel.

In 1937–42, the hotel began to be converted to the NeSoDak Bible Camp, and the hotel building and several small cabins were rented out. The nearby sheep shed became the Boy Scouts pony shed.

Some say the apparitions of Native American warriors can still be seen wandering the land, seeking revenge for their deaths. Native artifacts and arrowheads can still be found on the property.

PUNISHED WOMAN LAKE

In Codington County near South Shore there is a beautiful 477-acre lake with a horrible past. Early pioneers located two strange rock formations three miles south of the lake. Local Native Americans had created a 13-foot outline of a man's body, lying on the ground on his back with arms outstretched, using 104 large boulders. Nearby was another rock formation in the shape of a smaller female. These rock formations were constructed to document the local legend of the Punished Woman.

A beautiful Native American maiden named We-Wa-Ke was desired by many men, but she had eyes for only one man: Black Bear, the son of Big Eagle. After many attempts to win over We-Wa-Ke's father with gifts (that were denied) from Big Eagle, Black Bear became discouraged. The maiden's father wanted him to marry his sixty-year-old friend, White Tail Wolf. We-Wa-Ke obviously had no desire to marry the old man but was forced to do so for the sake of the tribe.

After the marriage, We-Wa-Ke and Black Bear decided to run away together and leave their tribes behind. Angry, White Tail Wolf had the young couple hunted down and captured. White Tail Wolf had We-Wa-Ke tied to a tree for punishment, while he stabbed her lover to death. Then he pointed his bow and arrow at We-Wa-Ke and shot her in the heart, killing her.

After he massacred the couple, White Tail Wolf looked upward toward the sky and yelled, "Evil Spirits take these two lovers to the Land of Everlasting Sorrow!" But the Great Spirit did not listen to White Tail Wolf's demand. Instead, the Great Spirit sent a lightning bolt down to the land, which struck White Tail Wolf, killing him instantly for his bad deeds.

The restless spirits of We-Wa-Ke and Black Bear can still be seen near the water's edge during the harvest moon.

LAKE KAMPESKA

Near Watertown, near Stony Point, there is another tragic Native American legend of a beautiful maiden named Minnequa (Laughing Maiden). The Natives called Lake Kampeska "Lake of the Shining Shells."

Minnequa (also spelled Minnecotah) was extremely beautiful. All the local warriors wished to have her hand in marriage, but she was in love with a

Wahpeton hunter named Wawaneta, who was battling competing tribes in a small village near Sisseton.

To stall for time until Wawaneta returned and ward off an unwanted marriage, Minnequa declared a challenge. "I will marry the man who can throw a large rock the farthest out into the lake!" she announced.

Many men accepted the challenge, and soon, they were all throwing the largest rocks they could find out into the water. One by one, these rocks were flung, and soon, a small island began to take shape. The men decided that Minnequa was playing a joke on them, and they became incredibly angry. They kidnapped the beautiful maiden and thrust her into a canoe. They paddled out to the small rock isle that they had built during the challenge and left her there to die from starvation. The men called the mound of rocks Maiden's Isle.

After dropping her off with only the clothes on her back, the men paddled away back toward land. Minnequa prayed to the Great Spirit to save her. Her prayers were soon answered when a huge white pelican began bringing her artichokes, berries and fish, saving her from starving to death.

Another chief named Osconee was dazzled by the brightness of the shining shells that were scattered along the lake shore and demanded that his men take him to the isle. When he arrived, he spotted the beautiful maiden alone on the rocks, and he instantly fell in love with her, demanding she become his wife. But Minnequa refused. This angered Osconee, and he became furious. No one denied him! He raised his bow and arrow, threatening to kill her, but the other warriors intervened and calmed him down.

Osconee was furious. "You shall starve upon these rocks, and I shall watch the hawks pick your bones!" he yelled at her. Little did he know she was being protected by the great pelican.

Osconee canoed back to shore, and night after night, he waited for the maiden to come to her senses and marry him. But her true love, Wawaneta, soon returned from Sisseton with his band of brave warriors. When he heard of the chief threatening his love, he became furious. Wawaneta's warriors attacked and fought Osconee and his men, until all of them were dead or driven away. Wawaneta quickly canoed out to the sacred isle and rescued Minnequa. The lovers ran off together to live a quiet life away from the tribe.

No one ever knows what happened to Minnequa and Wawaneta. Their disappearance remains a mystery to this day. Did they really live a quiet life, or did Osconee's men capture the lovers and kill them both out of revenge?

Stony Point was once a Native American campsite, and many wonderful artifacts can still be found on the grounds.

A pelican saved Minnequa from starving to death by bringing her berries and fish until her lover, Wawaneta, could rescue her. *Courtesy of LOC, drawn from nature by John James Audubon, 1836, #92517334.*

Lake Tetonkaha

Farther south near Brookings is a body of water called Lake Tetonkaha. The legend of its separation has been told and retold for many years. A local Native American chief knew he had the most beautiful daughter in his tribe. Many warriors wished to marry her. "I will give my daughter to the strongest brave who can paddle the fastest across the lake. The challenge begins at midnight!" the chief announced.

As pretty as his daughter was, only two young men accepted the challenge. This concerned the chief greatly, as he knew one was a good man and the other was known to be cruel.

At midnight, the two braves were inside their canoes ready to paddle the long distance across the lake. Sneering, the cruel boy had secretly damaged his challenger's boat. Somehow, the young maiden knew the cruel one had done something sinister; she demanded the kind boy use her canoe instead. She did not want to marry a man of bad character.

As the chief announced the start of the race, all eyes were on the two boys. All watched in astonishment as the noble boy paddled his canoe across the water. Magically, the lake was splitting into two. This division of the waters formed the narrow waterway that still exists today.

The kind and gentle brave won the hearts and respect of all the villagers, including the chief and the beautiful maiden. Naturally, he won the challenge. It was never told what happened to the conniving brave.

Burial Mounds

Strange mounds can be found throughout South Dakota and especially near Lake Tetonkaha and the Oakwoods Lakes area, where ten mysterious mounds have been found. The mounds are about three to six feet high and over one hundred feet in diameter. They date to AD 300 to AD 1400.

Who was responsible for creating these mounds, no one really knows. Relics from the mound builders can be found scattered around the land, such as pieces of pottery, stones used as hammers and objects similar to arrowheads.

When excavated, the mounds have been found to contain human remains. Burial practices and rituals are common among many cultures. Archaeologists discovered that some of the skeletons were buried and were never moved. Others, oddly, may have been hanged and then taken to the mounds. These bodies were often wrapped in skin, bark or other types of coverings. Some mounds contained only a single skeleton, whereas some of the others held multiple bodies.

Who actually made these mounds? Why did they not bury their dead deep in the ground? Some people have seen glowing orbs hovering over these mysterious burial mounds. Could it be an illusion or something paranormal?

LONG LAKE AND GOLD COINS

The legend of Long Lake, Gray Foot and his sack of gold coins has been retold since 1862. The 350-acre lake is located in Marshall County, northwest of Aberdeen.

During the Sioux Uprising in 1862, hundreds of people were murdered, and there was much animosity between the Whites and the Sioux tribes. During the uprising in Minnesota, a group of Santee Sioux raided the Indian Agency in Martin, Minnesota, where they killed and scalped several U.S. soldiers. Their loot? It was payroll time, and gold coins were stacked on the table inside the agency.

After the Sioux killed the soldiers, they grabbed as many gold coins as they could carry. Gray Foot, one of the Sioux, filled a flour sack he had on hand with approximately $56,000 in gold coins. He ran back to his horse, tied the coins to his steed and galloped off.

When representatives of the War Department arrived on the bloody scene, they were furious. They put out a bulletin stating, "Anyone found with gold coins in his possession will be promptly hanged!" How many of the gold coins were recovered remains a mystery.

In 1910, Gray Foot became ill. On his deathbed, he confessed to his sons about the murders and the stolen gold coins. "I buried the gold near the east end of Long Lake, by the two straight willows, on the lake's east shore," he whispered. Where exactly the gold coins are buried remains a mystery. They have never been located. Today, the coins would be worth $1,668,023—not including their historical value.

Gray Foot's ghostly apparition can still be seen wandering the shoreline, in the hopes of finding his lost gold.

Red Iron Lake Skeletons

The fall of 1922 brought a bit of a surprise to workers digging near State Highway 10 just east of Red Iron Lake. Red Iron Lake is located in central Marshall County, South Dakota. As their equipment hit what appeared to be human remains, work halted. When the authorities arrived, a total of five skeletons were unearthed. But who were these people buried off the side of the highway?

It was confirmed that the grave was very shallow, less than two feet deep, in the sandy loam. This would indicate that perhaps it was hastily done. Sandy soil is easier to dig in than soil that's hard and compact.

The police searched their old-school databases and files but were not able to locate any missing persons in the area.

There was one more gruesome detail: the skeletal remains were all children. One lonely clue was left among the bones: a single laced shoe. The bodies were removed and given a proper burial.

Locals believed that early immigrants to the area had possibly lost their children to disease, a tragedy or fire and buried them in the sandy mound. Since DNA analysis was not invented until the 1980s, it would have been impossible for the police and coroners to identify the deceased children.

The workers had discovered another small skeleton tucked inside a wooden box earlier that year.

The restless souls of these unknown children may still be wandering the shores of Red Iron Lake today, playing in the water, laughing, skipping rocks—tiny luxuries that were, sadly, stolen from them at an early age.

CHAPTER 4
MONSTERS AND MYSTERIES

Monsters are real, and ghosts are real, too.
They live inside us, and sometimes, they win.
—*Stephen King*

THE LEGEND OF THE TAKU-HE, SOUTH DAKOTA'S BIGFOOT

For generations, many have believed they have encountered a mysterious creature known as Bigfoot. In South Dakota, some call this monster the Taku-He. In April 1986, several teenagers reported hearing very frightening, indescribable sounds coming from deep within a forest in Brown County. The teenagers were so distraught that they made an official police report. It is no wonder the teens were frightened. In the late 1970s, several teenagers who were hiking in the woods went missing, never to be found. Their disappearances occurred shortly after multiple Taku-He sightings were reported in the woods. Did the teens really meet up with the legendary beast? Or was it an act of foul play?

Descriptions of the beast are the usual: an oversized, hairy, manlike beast that smells bad. But the South Dakota Taku-He is said to have been seen dragging dead carcasses behind it.

Cattle mutilations have also been reported after sightings of a Taku-He. During the 1970s, over twenty-five Taku-He sightings were reported by Mrs. Phoebe Little Dog in a pasture near Little Eagle in Corson County, left of Aberdeen. Cecelia Thunder Shield and Dan Uses Arrow both saw the monster twice as they were foraging for mushrooms in a nearby pasture. They claimed the creature's arms were so long, they could touch its ankles. The women ran as fast as they could the one-mile distance to Albert Dog's house, where they told the story of their harrowing adventure.

The sightings continued, and many skeptics got on board with capturing the creature when it showed up three hundred yards from the Little Eagle School. As word spread of the children's vulnerability, fourteen armed men and two officers from the Bureau of Indian Affairs, Verdell Veo and Gary Alexander, banned together to search for the beast. Their combined efforts were both on horseback and on ATVs. Cecelia Thunder Shield, Dan Uses Arrow and Albert Dog all ran back to the trading post to alert the others.

Albert Dog went running as fast as he could to see if he could catch up to the monster, but after a quarter of a mile, he lost the beast.

On searching, the group found many large tracks near the river. They believed the creature must have crossed the water to safety. Sadly, a bird hunter, Leonard Coop, found a teen's body down in a ravine a few weeks later. No autopsy reports can be located for the teen.

THE EERIE SOUNDS OF high-pitched shrieks are often heard by neighbors (similar to the sound of an elephant trumpeting), followed by their dogs howling and barking incessantly. Unusual footprints have even been found and measured by locals. They are noted as being eighteen inches long by eight wide. Another local claimed to have spotted the ginormous beast in a cow pasture. It was chasing the cows and appeared to be about two hundred yards behind the bovines.

When a local teenager, Elvis Flying By, went missing on October 4, 1977, his disappearance was blamed on Taku-He.

On October 28, the same year, an elderly woman, Mrs. Hanna Shooting Bear, spotted a mysterious, hairy creature looking into her neighbor's window in the trailer park. She screamed. Another neighbor, hearing the scream, came running out to see what the commotion was about. When he spotted the beast, he shot his rifle up into the air, firing six shots, hoping to scare the beast away.

Some say the small town drummed up the complaints for publicity, as Little Eagle was becoming nationally recognized due to the sightings. But none of the townspeople seemed to have struck it rich from the stories of the beast. And Veo himself, a well-respected officer for the Bureau of Indian Affairs, told the press that he had seen the creature with his very own eyes.

So are the residents of Little Eagle still spotting the hairy beast? Or have the mysterious sightings died down? If the eight-foot-tall beast still haunts and tortures Little Eagle, no one is talking about it.

NOTE: Many Bigfoot sightings in South Dakota are still occurring. There have been nineteen reported sightings just in the past year. Bear in mind that many sightings go unreported.

THE MONSTER AT SICA HOLLOW

Another Bigfoot-style story is the Legend of Sica Hollow. Sica Hollow (pronounced *she-cha*) is about fifteen miles northwest of Sisseton. It is said that the streams at Sica Hollow run blood red and rotting tree stumps glow an unusual color of green at night.

But what is the creature that roams Sica Hollow, haunting the forests? Other paranormal activities occur in the area, such as the sounds of Native American drums, screeching and whooping and late-night sightings of the ghosts of Native warriors. The Natives called the area Sica, which translates to *bad* or *evil*. But why?

A strange man appeared one day at the Natives' camp. He said his name was Hand. He wore tattered clothes. He had no family. He made the young maidens nervous, and the elders wanted him to leave. But the chief had a soft heart and told them that the weather was below freezing, Big Stone Lake was solid ice and Hand should be allowed to stay until the spring thaw.

When spring came, Hand had other plans. He lured the young warriors with tales of teaching them better hunting skills, which, in turn, would land them wives. But Hand taught the young warriors more sinister skills, too— like how to kill people.

When a clan was traveling by the Natives' camp, the young warriors attacked the innocent people and killed them all. Whooping and hollering in their bloody frenzy, they were shunned by their own people. A dark curse fell upon the tribe for the bloody battle. It is said that the ghosts of these tricked warriors still roam the land, seeking revenge on Hand and forgiveness from their people.

Some locals say there is a secret entrance to a hidden forest in Sica that only a select few know about. Others claim a Bigfoot haunts the forest.

The Legend of Sica Hollow claims that the streams run blood red and rotting tree stumps in the forest glow an unusual shade of green at night. *Courtesy of LOC, Russell Lee, photographer, 1942, #2017818874.*

The legend gets even more mysterious and creepy when it is coupled with the true story of several local hikers who went missing as they were exploring Sica Hollow in the late 1970s. Perhaps the hikers met up with foul play, or perhaps they fell victim to the many known spots of quicksand in the area.

The Trail of Spirits is said to be hauntingly beautiful but excessively creepy. Some claim to have seen strange lights and gurgling water that sometimes appears red like blood and heard the faint sounds of drums and bizarre howling sounds. Some believe Sica Hollow was cursed by Native Americans.

Sica Hollow State Park is open for horseback riding, camping and picnicking. Just be careful you do not get spooked by strange sounds and waters that run blood red.

NOTE: The Trail of the Spirits is located at Sica Hollow State Park, 44950 Park Road, Sisseton. Directions: From Sisseton, drive west on Highway 10/119th Street Turn right (north) on Sica Hollow Road/447th Avenue. It will curve to the left before you turn north on County Highway 10 and drive into Sica Hollow State Park.

The Legend of the Thunder Horses

Another mythological creature special to South Dakota was the Thunder Horse. The Sioux tribes were unique to the Santee Dakota territory, which encompassed North and South Dakota, Minnesota and northern Iowa. They retold the legend of the Thunder Horses to the young warriors, passing down the story for many years around the bonfire. But was the creature mythological?

Stories of the Thunder Horses led back all the way to the 1600s. The Native Americans claimed they were giant horses that moved up to live in the sky. When they got hungry, they would come down to chase the bison. The horses were so heavy that when they hit the earth, they shook the ground, creating a sound similar to thunder. As they chased the bison, their speed would create a massive storm, and eventually, the icy storm would cause the Thunder Horses to fall, their bones becoming stones. These horse-bone stones would later be gathered by the Sioux as relics and taken back to their camps.

In 1875, a paleontologist, Othniel Marsh, wanted to see if there was any truth to the legend of the Thunder Horses. He gathered his troop and came

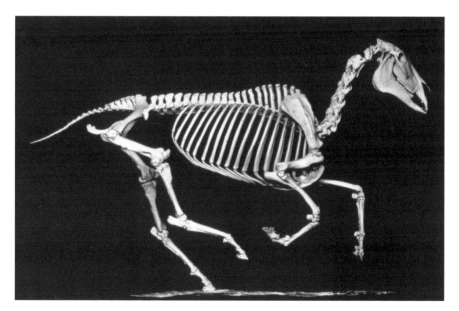

The legend of Thunder Horse was based on the bones of a Megacerops, a rhinoceros-like horse from thirty-eight million years ago. *Courtesy of LOC, Eadweard Muybridge, photographer, 1881, #2009631282.*

to the Dakotas. A Sioux leader showed him a massive jawbone he said came from a Thunder Horse. Marsh could not believe his eyes. The molar was a whopping three inches wide! Excited, his group began excavating bones they believed were those of the Thunder Horses. After some digging, incredibly, the team unearthed an entire skeleton. The creature was eight feet tall at the withers, about sixteen feet long and had a *Y*-shaped horn on its head and four toes on each foot/hoof. After some research, Marsh discovered that the unearthed Thunder Horse was actually a Megacerops, a rhinoceros-style horse from thirty-eight million years ago.

What is interesting about the legend of the Thunder Horse is that the Sioux were not around thirty-eight million years ago—so the legend probably was a way of explaining the strange bones. It makes one wonder about other hauntings, legends and lore that are passed down—are many of them true and they just have not been proven yet?

ENORMOUS SNAKELIKE CREATURE IN BIG STONE LAKE

In 1886, an unusual report of a huge snake swimming around in Big Stone Lake scared the locals. Thomas O'Neal, a woodchopper, felled a tree near the old Smith Ashley ranch (three miles from Concord). As he and his help were cleaning up the job, he noticed something out of the corner of his

In 1886, an unusual report of a two-hundred-pound snake swimming around in Big Stone Lake scared the locals. *Courtesy of LOC #2006682672.*

eye. As he peered closer, he was shocked at what he saw: a type of snakelike creature that he believed measured a whopping fourteen feet long with a head three feet around that was shaped like a crocodile's. The men saw it had light-colored skin with odd patches of hair on its body. O'Neal thought the creature had eight pairs of webbed feet and probably weighed about two hundred pounds.

The strange creature swam away, leaving the men frightened and stunned. They thought it may have curled itself up inside a hollowed-out part of a tree near the water. The men quickly ran back up the shore, leaving their coats and hats behind in their haste.

Back in town, the men rallied, and after much thought, they figured the creature was some sort of amphisbaena typically living in South America. How in the world would a snake from South America end up in Big Stone Lake? It was a mystery.

The largest snake species in the United States is the eastern indigo—but even so, that species can only get up to eleven pounds and about nine feet long. The next possibility is a misplaced Burmese python—which can be up to two hundred pounds and twenty-three feet long! But how a snake found only in another country got into Big Stone is certainly a mystery.

Big Stone Lake covers 12,610 acres, is 26 miles long and flows 332 miles into the Mississippi River. *Courtesy of author.*

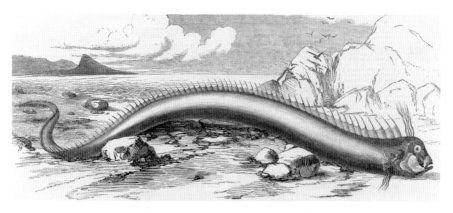

In 1886, an unusual report of a huge snake, like the one pictured, swimming around in Big Stone Lake scared the locals. *Courtesy of LOC, a sketch by W.D. Munro, Bermuda Islands, 1860, #2001695531.*

Did it somehow get trapped and carried to South Dakota on a boat? Big Stone Lake covers 12,610 miles, is 26 miles long and around 1 mile wide. It flows 332 miles into the Mississippi River. Could some strange reptile have slithered its way through the murky waters to make its home off the bank of the lake in town? Highly unlikely.

Since O'Neal and his men were of sound mind and good reputations, it is also highly unlikely that they made the story up for attention. And why did it have the body of a snake and the head of a crocodile? Was it some sort of mutation? So what exactly was the mysterious creature they spotted in 1886? To this day, it remains an unsolved mystery.

WEREWOLVES ON THE PRAIRIES

The legend of the werewolf dates back as far as the fifteenth century. The oldest evidence of man-to-wolf shapeshifting dates to 2100 BC, but the werewolf as we now know it today first appeared in ancient Greece. The creature is believed to have a lifespan of thousands of years. The creature today is believed to be a human that magically transforms into a mythological beast resembling a huge wolf that feeds on livestock. Some records indicate that werewolves are not against killing and mutilating humans or even children.

The full moon adds to the beast's aggressiveness. This additional aggressiveness is not a fallacy. A study conducted at Australia's Calvary Mater Newcastle hospital discovered that a full moon brings out the "beast" in many types of humans. The study found that in just one year, of the ninety-one recorded violent incidents they dealt with, 23 percent of them occurred during a full moon.

But why? Some believe it is because our bodies are made up of 60 percent water and the direct magnetic pull from the moon to the Earth can create an agitated state in a person. Other medical conditions that may suggest werewolf-type behaviors and unique physical appearances are lycanthropy (a psychological condition that makes people believe they are changing into wolves), hypertrichosis (a genetic disorder causing excessive hair growth, creating the illusion of becoming a werewolf), rabies and hallucination caused by drugs.

Historically, many believed that the only way to kill a "werewolf" was to burn it at the stake. In actuality, most of these werewolves were not shapeshifters at all but instead serial killers or mentally insane individuals.

South Dakota has been home to several local werewolves, dating as far back as 1906. A farmer named F.M. Bennett was tired of his cattle and hogs being attacked and killed during the middle of the night. He went on a mission to solve his problem—with rifle in hand. After a few more deadly incidents, Bennett's nerves were on his last straw. He soon came upon the beast. He figured the creature measured at least six feet long. The head of the mysterious wolflike animal was over a foot long. Frightened but determined, Bennett raised his rifle and quickly shot it a few times. He proudly mounted the beast and showed off his capture of the bizarre, oversized wolf to anyone that would come see it!

Another werewolf-type haunting was recorded in 1923 near De Smet. This ruthless creature was responsible for killing hundreds of local cattle and pigs. The farmers were losing money, and they had all lost patience with the bloodthirsty creature. One man alone had lost an incredible seventy-plus hogs from his farm to this particular animal.

They gathered, each man with a gun or rifle in hand, and piled into a large, old Buick. Several hunting dogs were also in the back seat, frothing at the mouth. They drove through the fields at over thirty miles per hour, carefully following the large wolf-beast. The pack of dogs was out of control in a mad frenzy and, without warning, jumped through the windows of the car, shattering the glass.

The hysteria heightened as the dogs began chasing the oversized wolf-animal. The smaller dogs were faster than the gigantic creature and were

Order–Carnivora.
Family–Dogs

GRAY WOLF
CANIS LUPUS

¾ Natural Size
Northern Hemisphere

In 1923, a werewolf-type haunting was recorded near De Smet. The creature measured five feet, six inches in length and weighed over 150 pounds. *Courtesy of LOC, L. Prang & Company, 1874, #2017660731.*

soon able to attack it. The men, Charles Cummins, Joseph Henkel and Joseph Brown, were not far behind and took to shooting at the wolf when it was safe to do so.

When the werewolf-style creature was dead, they approached it cautiously. It had a black coat rather than the typical gray found on wolves in that area. They concurred that this wolf-beast was the largest recorded east of the Missouri River. Its body measured five foot six inches in length, and it weighed over 150 pounds.

THE LEGEND OF THREE TOES

Another true story of a wolf creature is the legend of Three Toes. In the early 1920s, a huge beast was terrorizing South Dakota and other nearby states. Many ranchers were losing their stock to what appeared to be an oversized, but uncommonly intelligent, wolf. Three Toes was killing cows, sheep and horses in record numbers. Some locals claimed Three Toes had killed over fifty thousand animals in a brief period, the creature was so bloodthirsty.

But Three Toes seemed to possess strange habits and thought patterns. Some believed that Three Toes was an escaped sleigh dog that came down from Canada, because at times, the animal appeared to crave human contact. Some farmers thought Three Toes moved more like a man than a beast, and he could outsmart almost any hunter.

In 1909, a local rancher named Charley Wilson spotted Three Toes on his land. When he inspected the animal's tracks, he noticed the beast only had three toes on his front foot (which is how he acquired his nickname). He thought the wolf creature was probably two years old at the time. Three Toes continued to consume any animals he felt fit his needs.

The following year, Eric Haivala's stock was being killed. The local ranchers set out multiple traps, hoping to kill the beast once and for all. Instead, Haivala and his neighbors only got another toe from him: a bloody digit left in the jaws of a trap. In retaliation, Three Toes attacked more of Haivala's stock. What was most peculiar was that the farmers noticed only cows with the Haivala brand on them were being killed. How did Three Toes know which cows to slaughter in revenge? Again, the beast displayed an unusual amount of intelligence.

In 1912, a dozen lambs were killed in another field. Three Toes' unique prints were found nearby.

Finally, a handsome reward was offered for the capture of Three Toes. Many men thought they could outsmart the creature, but they all came back empty handed. They, too, believed Three Toes was unusually smart.

The local ranchers realized that Three Toes had gotten himself a mate, as they saw him roaming with a she-wolf. In 1920, Three Toes' female counterpart was caught in a trap and died. Three Toes went on a murderous rampage. He tore through thirty-four of a local farmer's sheep in a single night. Then he killed another twenty-four lambs and another seventeen the following week.

In 1922, a farmer named Lehti purchased twenty-four registered bucks for $3,500. It was not long before Three Toes slaughtered them all.

When the Haivala boys discovered yet another dead cow, they decided enough was enough. They stuffed the dead cow with poison, knowing Three Toes only dined on fresh meat. They watched in awe as Three Toes returned to his kill, tore out a piece of bloody meat, then spit it out of his mouth. He looked the boys straight in the eye as if to say, "I am smarter than you."

Three Toes' strength was legendary. He was once spotted carrying half a horse in his mouth about seventy-five feet, without ever letting the carcass touch the ground! (An average horse weighs about 1,200 pounds.) His cast-iron stomach was also perplexing. It was noted that Three Toes once ate twelve chunks of poison and was not affected by it. Three Toe's agility was also fascinating. Ranchers who were trying to trap the beast witnessed him leaping across a thirty-foot-wide ditch!

The state was fed up with the werewolf's actions. Officials hired four professional hunters from four different states to track down and kill Three Toes. The men quickly located Three Toes, and although the men were excellent shooters and sixteen shots were fired, Three Toes ran away without so much as a scratch.

In 1923, an expert hunter named John Martin was hired by the state to take on the challenge of capturing Three Toes. He tracked Three Toes for three days and covered two hundred miles of terrain. Martin could tell the beast was getting tired, and he felt the reward would soon be his. But Three Toes outsmarted him: he began walking on patches of ice so that he could not be tracked.

Three Toes was once seen just a few feet away from a house, staring longingly and peacefully into the windows. This strange behavior only added to the myth that the animal was possibly, at one time, a man and he was remembering his life as such. Could Three Toes have actually been a human at one time, and for some odd reason, he was turned into a wolf, as legend states? How?

The locals were getting desperate. Master hunter Clyde Briggs was next called to the scene all the way from Washington, D.C. He was determined to capture and kill Three Toes so farmers could finally live without the fear of their herds being eaten. Briggs assembled thirteen sets of traps and used various other methods to try to capture Three Toes. After a few weeks, on July 23, 1925, Three Toes' reign of terror was finally over. He had finally been trapped. When Briggs came upon the beast, he noted that Three Toes offered no resistance, even when he wired the animal's snout shut. He raised his gun to put the beast out of his misery, but then thought better of it. He decided to take the creature back to the city alive for everyone to see.

With the help of several men, Three Toes was loaded into the back of Briggs's vehicle. But Three Toes' spirit had been taken from him. He traveled silently and solemnly. He never put up a fight. He slowly closed his eyes and died before Briggs could reach the city. Some say Three Toes died from a broken heart at his final capture.

Did Three Toes actually know what the plans were for his final days and simply will himself to die instead? Why did Three Toes possess such human capabilities and knowledge? No one will ever know.

So what were these werewolf-type creatures? Were they simply mutants of the common wolf or something more sinister?

LIVESTOCK MUTILATIONS

One of the most horrifying and mysterious occurrences is the senseless mutilation of livestock. South Dakota ranchers have experienced these tragic attacks for many decades, with the highest number of occurrences during the 1970s.

In 1974, over twenty-one formal complaints were filed in just two weeks! Some farmers believed these injuries were caused by devil worshippers or were simply gruesome pranks played out by inconsiderate teenagers. On inspection, the dead calves' and cattle's lips, ears, tails and tongues had been

In the 1970s, over fifty complaints were filed about cattle mutilations in South Dakota. Some cows curiously appeared to have been "dropped from the air." Others were mutilated like the cow depicted in this painting. *Courtesy of LOC, Bernard Joseph Steffen, artist, #91785031.*

removed with precise cuts. Little to no blood was found at the site. How can a dismemberment occur but leave no blood? Also, no tracks (animal or human) were found near the dead cows. Surely, teenagers would leave some sort of footprints nearby.

Soon, other cattle mutilation reports began to pour in, in Kansas, Nebraska and Iowa. One farmer claimed to have seen an unidentified flying object just a little while prior to one of his cattle being killed. In northeast South Dakota, particularly Day and Roberts Counties, more reports were filed. One rancher told investigators he believed one of his six-hundred-pound calves was somehow "airlifted," then laid back down in his pasture. He also said there were no tracks found anywhere and no evidence of an automobile or truck. A nineteen-year-old girl claimed her prize cow had been mutilated in the same manner but that its jaw had also been removed. The cow also had three four-inch-deep punctures and a triangular pattern on its body.

Dr. Mahlon Vorhies, a professor of veterinary sciences at South Dakota State University, was called in to examine ten of the carcasses and give his professional opinion. "We suspect that more than predators are involved. They have not died from disease; they have been mutilated."

By the end of 1974, up to fifty cases had been reported. Many more attacks probably happened but were not reported for fear of ridicule. Ranchers were getting frustrated. Each cow killed cost them big money. They demanded answers.

Since the incisions were done with surgical precision, that ruled out predators like coyotes and bears. There were never any footprints or tire tracks left behind, so that would rule out humans.

Over the years, there have been over ten thousand reported cases of livestock mutilations around the United States. When examined, many of the cows had severe bruising and broken bones as if they were dropped from a great height. An average adult cow weighs between 1,600 and 2,400 pounds. How could an animal of that weight be lifted up by some invisible force?

What is even more bizarre is that natural, hungry predators will not get close to these carcasses and typically stay more than twenty feet away! But why?

Myron Scott, a South Dakota rancher, was out feeding his cows hay one night when he noticed strange lights hovering in the sky over his pasture. The next morning, when he went to look after his herd, he noticed one of his cows was dead. The hide of the animal had been pulled up and over its body, like a cigar roll. The animal's tongue had been removed. Its horns and

Over ten thousand cases of livestock mutilation have been recorded in the United States. Many mutilated cows had little to no blood left in them. *Courtesy of LOC, Carol M. Highsmith, photographer, #2011635768.*

spine were broken, as if it had been dropped from the sky. There was no blood and no tracks.

In the late 1970s and 1980s, ranchers in twenty-two states began reporting mutilations on their farms, from Oregon to Florida. Colorado was hit the hardest, with a whopping 1,500 documented cases. Of these, only ten cows were determined to have been killed by human hands.

Frustrated, Rio Blanco County officials offered a $25,000 reward was offered for information leading to the arrest of people involved in the attacks. As police and professors studied over two hundred photographs submitted to them, they quickly determined that natural predators did not do the killings.

A particularly unusual case involved farmers Jim and Helen Edwards. One of their dead cows was examined, and it was discovered that the cow died from "a fall from a very high elevation." The Edwardses were left scratching their heads, as there were no cliffs or mountains anywhere on their property.

In 1979, Anthony Whirlwind Horse of the Bureau of Indian Affairs was brought in to investigate mutilations on the Pine Ridge Reservation. Multiple times, he was called out to examine dead cows that were found lying on their backs with all four legs pointing straight up into the air. Their organs had been removed with a surgical instrument.

Near Sisseton, six steers were found dead on Don Stickle's farm. Each weighed approximately nine hundred pounds. Their ears, lips, eyes and sex organs had all been removed.

In Wilmot, South Dakota, a four-hundred-pound young bull owned by Ray Hanson was slain. Tests run by South Dakota State University showed the mutilated cows had little to no blood left in them.

Also in South Dakota, in 1993, a longtime farmer in De Smet, Art Geyer, had one of his expensive Charolais bulls and two cows killed tragically. "It was unlike anything I have ever seen," he said. The bull's penis and testes had been surgically removed, along with ears and tongue. No blood was found at the scene.

What is causing the deaths of these animals? Is it aliens, witches, paranormal activity, natural predators or something even more evil?

THE UNKILLABLE MAN

A South Dakota man who traveled all over the state became well-known as impossible to kill and a bit of a mystery in the area. David Wakefield had a rough-and-tumble kind of life. He was an intelligent man who always seemed to be lucky, too.

Three times, Wakefield had encountered foul play and was shot—and all three times, left for dead—yet he somehow, magically, survived. Four times, the local doctor told him to get his things in order, for he was not long in this world—but all four times, Wakefield miraculously survived and conquered his severe illnesses. Another time, he fell from a hundred-foot cliff, bounced off a tree and landed on his feet, much like a cat—without a scratch on him.

Later in life, Wakefield got into another scuffle and shot a man dead. The judge did not take much time in deliberation, and when he asked Wakefield if he wanted a lawyer, Wakefield's answer surprised the judge: "I had been a lawyer earlier in my life and can very well represent myself, but all I really want to do is rest in a grave."

Wakefield had his wish granted. "David Wakefield, you will be hanged from the neck until you are dead!" the judge stated.

In September 1909, Wakefield was promptly deeded legally and physically dead by the coroner, taken down from the rope and buried in the local cemetery. The entire town commented that that would be the last time they would see the Unkillable David Wakefield alive. Boy, were they wrong!

Late that night, an aspiring doctor, wishing to examine the body for medical purposes and valuable insight into the workings of the human body, carefully dug up Wakefield's grave, removed the body and took it back to his practice, where he planned to dissect it. After the doctor placed the body on his examining table, he left the room to gather his instruments. During the brief period of the doctor's absence, Wakefield's body slowly came to life from the warmth of the room. Much to the doctor's shock, Wakefield was sitting in a chair drinking water when he returned.

Knowing that he had been buried without any money, Wakefield took the strange opportunity to bribe the doctor. "If you give me one hundred dollars, I will not tell the authorities about your illegal graverobbing practices!"

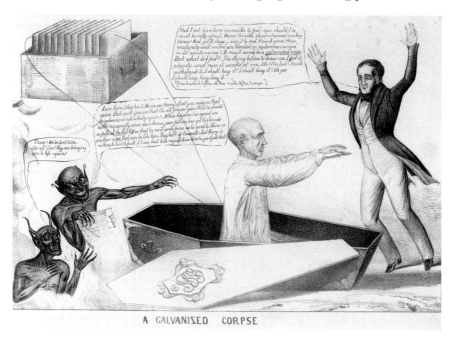

A GALVANISED CORPSE

In 1909, David Wakefield's corpse was stolen from his grave by a medical doctor. He mysteriously came back to life and even testified at his own murder trial. Before embalming, people were sometimes buried alive. *Courtesy of LOC, drawing by Henry R. Robinson, 1836, #2008661296.*

"How dare you!" the doctor exclaimed. "I will not!"

Wakefield proceeded to leave the man's house and wander into the street. The next morning, he walked back to the judge and exclaimed, "Your honor, I am legally a corpse, and this case must go to trial on such grounds. Death, according to the law, separates a man from all his earthly possessions except his body." Knowing the law, Wakefield continued. "It is a maxim of common law that there can be no property in a corpse—this is, no one living can own it. My corpse is my own property."

Opposing council was shocked. How could a legally dead man come back from the grave to give directions? "I claim," he stated, "that the plaintiff is Wakefield's *ghost*. Since he places his case on technicalities, I will do the same. Let him prove that he is not a disembodied spirit!"

Outsmarting the other lawyer, Wakefield concluded, "It is not necessary. The law takes no cognizance of ghosts. When a man is dead, the law says that he shall stay dead. His apparition has no standing in court."

Astonished, the judge and opposing council stood, jaws dropped.

The strange legal proceedings continued. "The law holds that the corpse, being the owner of itself before death, possesses certain rights over itself after it becomes dead. Every corpse has the inalienable right to six feet of ground to be buried in and the right of being buried….The corpse died on grounds under the authority of the courts. The courts buried it. The courts are responsible for its being left untouched in its grave."

The room remained in awe. Wakefield seemed as sharp as ever, either as his own ghost or his resurrected self. The opposing council was almost at a loss for words, as they had never seen a man defend his own corpse before.

Wakefield continued, "I admit that no living person has a right to recover for violation of sepulcher. That right is vested in the corpse. But in any previous cases, the corpse has not walked into the courtroom to claim its rights! A civil action may be brought for breaking and entering a place where a body is buried, the same as a trespass, for which damages can be recovered."

It seemed as though Wakefield had no intention of being brought back to life without his permission or without an exchange of money. The outwitted doctor also stood by, not knowing what to say.

"Having shown your honor that the defendant is only accountable to me, a corpse, and that he has willfully interfered with my rest in the grave, has brought me back to life is irksome to me, I ask that he be commanded by the court to pay me the damages claimed," Wakefield said.

The judge collapsed.

A nearby man stood up. "I am Judge Tatterton of the Supreme Court, traveling in your county. Permit me to say that the points stated by the plaintiff are legally correct in every particular."

The "corpse" of David Wakefield walked away with the $1,000 he demanded and also reimbursement for court costs.

So how was David Wakefield able to defy death multiple times over? How did he even survive being hanged and legally pronounced dead? How did he survive being buried six feet under without much air until the doctor dug up his grave? Was it the warmth of the doctor's examining room that did something to make Wakefield come back to life, or was it something more paranormal and spectacular?

It is unclear whatever happened to Wakefield after he received his money from the courts. Did he go on to live a long life? Perhaps he went back to work as a lawyer, continuing to dazzle the courtroom with his brilliance?

There are multiple, horrific stories about people accidentally being buried alive. Their bodies were later dug up to be moved or examined due to the suspicions of foul play—only for coroners to discover that their fingernails had been torn off by their frantic attempts to claw their way out. Clever morticians tried to rectify this problem by attaching a string to the dead one's wrist leading upward to a flag that would pop up to signal workers that they were still alive so they could quickly dig up the person before they ran out of air.

CHAPTER 5
OTHER HAUNTS AND HORRORS

Haunted places are like a bridge between the living and the past,
a realm where history still walks among us.
—Unknown

There are many other forms of hauntings and unexplained phenomena besides ghosts. Strange activities can include unnatural beings, bizarre monsters, gray men, unidentified flying objects in the sky, plasma, self-combustion and more. This chapter explores some of South Dakota's more sinister and unique experiences throughout the northeast part of the state.

MILBANK AND MURDERS

The small community of Milbank is known for its friendly residents, fun local activities and welcoming attitudes. The town was founded in 1880 when the Chicago, Milwaukee and St. Paul Railroad first laid track in South Dakota. Milbank was named after railroad director and successful businessman Jeremiah Milbank. The city was incorporated in 1894. Milbank is also the birthplace of the American Legion Baseball league, as it was first proposed at an American Legion state convention in Milbank, South Dakota, in 1925.

But who exactly were these citizens that worked so hard to make Milbank prosper? Are their names just lost to history? Unless someone goes out of their way to research directories and go through dusty records in the local historical society, many of these early pioneers will be forgotten forever.

Do any of the old-timers from the early 1900s haunt the historical buildings that still stand on Main Street? Does H.L. Smith, editor of the *Grant County Review* newspaper, still linger in the fabulous building where he once put ink to paper? Does Miss Shannon, the librarian at the Carnegie Library, still sit behind her desk making sure people return their books on time? Or how about C.D. Fairchild, the proprietor of the old Hotel St. Hubert on Main? Although the once-grand hotel has been demolished, does Fairchild linger on where his exquisite establishment once stood?

All these hardworking locals would be forgotten in time—perhaps that is why they choose to haunt places.

The small, somewhat sleepy town of Milbank possibly has multiple ghosts lingering in its midst. Many murders have been committed there over the years, the tragedies possibly trapping souls where the killings occurred. Some of the old buildings have been torn down and replaced; others remain not much different than when they were built. Why do trapped souls remain where they meet their demise? Why do some spirits decide to stay and others travel on to the next dimension? These are mysteries never to be answered.

But the quaint, quiet town has some disturbing incidents in its past, like most towns do. Do the restless ghosts of the victims still roam the streets of Milbank? Possibly.

Haunted Milbank Cemetery

A ghost story from Beth W.:

> *I often wander cemeteries. I find them fascinating. I just love the old tombstones! One time, I was wandering around the Milbank Cemetery, and I saw what appeared to be a man standing next to a grave. I did not see any other cars, so I figured he possibly walked there. But as quickly as he appeared, he disappeared! It startled me. I knew I had just seen a ghost!*

The unclaimed corpse of a man who was murdered (and whose body was stashed on top of a train that stopped in Milbank) is said to roam the Milbank Cemetery. His ghostly apparition can be spotted occasionally, as if it is confused. But who is this ghost?

During the early 1900s, many small towns were plagued with crime due to the influx of transients, hoboes and criminals who could easily travel via trains. When the Milwaukee Railroad laid down tracks in Milbank, problems increased in town.

One such incident took place on August 10, 1912. The bloody corpse of a murdered man was found on top of a passenger train car. A night operator at nearby Ortonville noticed blood on the train as it pulled out of the station. He quickly notified the Milbank depot, as that would be the train's next stop.

Ten miles later, when the train pulled into Milbank, officials were eagerly waiting. Officer Derrick crawled up onto the train's roof and saw the bloody body. He quickly summoned Justice A.J. Bleser to the scene. When they examined the corpse, they discovered its throat had been slit.

The train conductor wanted to get moving to stay on schedule, so the body was loaded onto a truck and placed in the baggage room at the depot. Newspaper reporter and *Grant County Review* owner William Dolan arrived at the baggage room. He thought the murder was very recent, as the corpse's flesh was still warm and blood was still dripping from the wound. Was the victim murdered in Ortonville, the train's last stop, or somewhere else?

Found on the body were a few dollars, some notes and names of ex-employers, an envelope with the name "Fred Kirchbaum of Granite Falls, Minnesota" written on it and a newspaper.

The officers soon came to discover that the man had been murdered in Correll, Minnesota, a small town a few miles before Ortonville. Officials in Correll spotted blood along the train tracks near their depot. The dead man's bloody hat was also lying by the tracks.

But who was the victim? Why was he murdered? When the police contacted some of the people in the victim's book, they discovered that he had worked for a man named H.E. Kopiska in North Dakota in 1909. Kopiska told officials that the victim was named Edward Riley and that Ed had worked for him for about six months.

When officials contacted the farmer whose name was on the envelope, Fred Kirchbaum, they were told the dead man had worked for him doing odd jobs for a few days. The farmer only knew the dead man's name was Ed and that he was a hard worker and good person. When the two men met up again so Kirchbaum could pay Ed the one hundred dollars owed for his labor, Ed told Kirchbaum that he was going to try to find work in Granite Falls, Minnesota, and if he could not, then he would head to Milbank in search of employment.

In 1912, a corpse was found on top of the passenger train car that stopped in Milbank at the train depot pictured here. *Courtesy of GCHS.*

Not finding work in Granite Falls, Ed had obviously boarded the train heading to Milbank. It was at this point that he met his horrible fate. Did someone kill Ed for his one hundred dollars? Eyewitnesses in Granite Falls told the police that Ed had been seen with a man who was claiming to repair umbrellas for a living, and he knew that Ed had one hundred dollars on him. Suspiciously, this umbrella repair man also boarded the train when Ed stepped aboard.

The police had their suspects, but no conviction for Edward Riley's murder was ever obtained. None of his relatives were ever located. After no further clues were revealed, the corpse of Ed Riley was buried in Milbank after a short prayer conducted by Reverend Haag.

Is the ghost that wanders the cemetery that of Riley, still looking for his killer? Tragic deaths often trap the souls of those murdered on Earth, and the person is unable to move on and into the light without help. Perhaps, someday, poor Ed's soul will give up and move to a happier place.

Murder of a Milbank Sheriff

The tragic murder of local sheriff Melbourne Lewis hit the small community of Milbank hard. The quiet town would soon learn of the senseless killing of their honorable police officer, and thousands would mourn.

The crime began on a warm afternoon, July 30, 1941. Reports of shots being fired in the Lake Farley vicinity flooded the sheriff's office. Who was this madman shooting in the park? Sheriff Lewis, Frank Miller and Ben Hughes rushed to the scene hoping to put a stop to the chaos.

When the men arrived, they noticed thick shrubs and bushes near a yard on Main Street—a perfect spot for some hoodlum to hide. Police chief John Farley also came to the scene to assist the other men in capturing the lunatic.

As the four men searched for the criminal, shots exploded into the air. The bullets were aimed at local businessman Ileen Nelson, who ran the Texaco service station. The bullet grazed Nelson but hit fourteen-year-old Lyle Tillemans, who was also watching the disturbance. (Tillemans would recover from the wound.)

The killer ran across Main Street and fled down toward the creek. Strangely, he then went into a neighbor's home and requested a drink of water. (He had hidden his rifle near some corn stalks before entering the home.) The murderer then ran to another service station and threw his gun under a nearby trailer house. Thirsty again, the killer went into the station, purchased two bottles of Coca-Cola and swiftly downed them.

Hearing of the murder and discovering the killer was on the loose, two more local men became involved in the manhunt: Harold Robel and Dr.

The killer of a Milbank sheriff ran into a service station like this one and quickly drank two bottles of Coca-Cola before he was captured. *Courtesy of LOC, Jack Delano, photographer, 1940, #2017791060.*

Clifford Hayes's mug shot after he was captured and sentenced to life in prison for killing Milbank sheriff Melbourne Lewis. *Courtesy of Sioux Falls State Penitentiary, reprinted in the* Rapid City Journal, *July 31, 1941.*

Gregory. A man at the station, J.T. Harvey, pointed at the strange thirsty man and indicated that he was the killer.

"Throw up your hands!" ordered Lewis.

"Go ahead and shoot!" answered the man. "You've got nothing on me!"

Sheriff Lewis was the man's next target. Without hesitation, he aimed and shot at the officers. A bullet hit Lewis square in the chest, killing him instantly. Lewis was only thirty-four years old at the time of his murder.

The killer was ordered to leave the service station by the remaining officers, which he did calmly and without any fight.

Once captured, the killer was identified as Clifford Hayes (also Haas). Hayes had just been released from the state penitentiary in Sioux Falls the day before. He arrived in Aberdeen with new overalls and a check for twenty-nine dollars issued by the state.

Hayes was in prison serving a twelve-year sentence for burglary. After only seven years and ten months, Hayes was released on good behavior. He had planned to hop on a train and head out to the West Coast. When a train never arrived, he waited in Aberdeen until he could sneak into a boxcar. That boxcar was headed toward Milbank. When he got off in Milbank at ten o'clock in the morning, he purchased a rifle and ammunition at the Milbank Gamble Store. Strangely, he had also bought a tie with some of the money. He desired to rob someone and wanted to wait until it was dark. Instead, he panicked and became a killer that afternoon.

Hayes was put up for adoption early in his life but lived a good home life with his new family. But for some reason, Hayes could never stay out of trouble. He was only thirty years old when he killed Lewis but had spent most of his adult life behind bars.

He pled not guilty, of course, to the cold-blooded killing of Lewis. He then changed his mind and agreed to his guilt. Then he changed his mind again. Back and forth, the man pleaded both his guilt and his innocence. He then confessed to killing Lewis and requested the death penalty. The judge quickly agreed, and his sentence in the electric chair was scheduled

Killer Clifford Hayes was to be executed in an electric chair, but instead, he got life in prison without parole. *Courtesy of LOC, 1908, #2012646356.*

for August 9, 1942. The problem with the sentence was that the county did not have an electric chair. One was borrowed for the grisly deed from Statesville Penitentiary in Joliet, Illinois. The chair was positioned in the Sioux Falls State Penitentiary, ready to shock Hayes to his death. If the punishment was carried out, Hayes would be the first person to be executed after capital punishment was reinstated in South Dakota, just two years prior to Lewis's murder.

But his death sentence would never be carried out. Hayes changed his mind again, and in 1943, he requested life in prison without parole. For some ridiculous reason, his request was granted, and the state would have to pay for his care and imprisonment for fifty-two years until 1993, when he finally died.

Lewis was well loved in the small town, and over two thousand went to his viewing at Mundwiler's Funeral Parlor. Does the soul of Lewis still wander Main Street in Milbank, seeking revenge for his untimely death in 1941?

The Hobo Murder

The small town of Milbank rarely experienced crime, let alone murder. But on a dark night in 1944, a horrific murder would occur, causing quite a stir among the locals. Joseph Hilts's body was found bludgeoned by a blunt object. The fifty-six-year-old man had gotten off the train in Milbank with another man, William Morgan. The two men had been traveling as hoboes, via the railroad.

At one time, Milbank had what was called a Hobo Jungle, situated northwest of the town's railroad yard near Lake Farley. The local hoboes were not bums; they were unemployed men eagerly searching for work. Milbank was a popular rest stop for hundreds of men. It provided a fire pit for cooking and a place to sleep, if need be. The group of hoboes was riding the Milwaukee Railroad boxcars heading West to hopefully secure work harvesting grain or picking fruit. Hilts and Morgan were two of these men.

After the Great Depression that caused such havoc from the late 1920s into the 1940s, countless families experienced severe financial troubles. Banks were collapsing; the stock market was crashing; people were losing their homes.

Friends Hilts and Morgan were on Main Street in Milbank, pictured here in the 1920s. They spent time in the Cozy Lane Billiard Parlor and Tavern before Hilt was murdered. *Courtesy of GCHS.*

The victim, Hilts, had no confidence in banks, so he was prone to carrying thousands of dollars' worth of cash tucked neatly into his money belt. This was probably the motive for his robbery and untimely death.

On August 7, 1944, Hilts and his friend Morgan were seen together walking down Main Street in Milbank. They casually spent some time in the Cozy Lane Billiard Parlor and Tavern. Then the two men popped into Fossum Shoe Store for some new bootstraps. What happened later that evening, we can only speculate.

When another hobo arrived later at the Jungle in Milbank, he noticed the camp was in disarray. Tin can cups were littered about the park, the kettle was overturned and other things seemed out of place.

Then he discovered the body of a dead man. The man had been beaten with some type of club and robbed of the majority of his money. The bloody corpse was Hilt.

The frightened man ran to the Milwaukee Railroad office to tell officials about the body. The railroad men quickly notified the police about the incident. They found one hundred dollars hidden in one of Hilt's pockets.

Sheriff Russel Griese, state's attorney Frank Tait and local coroner Doctor D.A. Gregory hurried to the crime scene. Although they did a thorough search, there were few helpful clues. The railroad did what they could and ordered the last train from Milbank held at Aberdeen so the officers could question those on board. But nothing concrete came from the interrogations.

A group of unidentified Milbank citizens enjoying the parade during Field Day on Main Street in 1908. *Courtesy of GCHS.*

Back in Milbank, the men questioned locals. Had they seen or heard anything out of place on the evening of the seventh? Did anyone know Hilts or Morgan?

Griese discovered that Hilts had a brother in Boone, Iowa. He told the officer that Hilts had been traveling west in hopes of finding work in Canada. The brother also admitted that Hilts was prone to carrying large amounts of cash on his person. He would routinely mark his bills in a unique manner.

Several states away, forty-two-year-old Morgan was working in the small town of Skykomish, Washington, removing the wreckage of a Great Northern train. Since he was actively spending the marked money he stole from Hilts, the FBI promptly arrested him on March 10, 1945, in Seattle, Washington. Morgan was tried, found guilty and sentenced to twenty-five years' hard labor at the state penitentiary.

Does Hilts's angry spirit still roam the old hobo railroad camp in Milbank? Some say yes.

The Bloody Barn

A local Milbank farmer, thirty-year-old Albert Wolf, had a place located just three miles southeast of town. Wolf was a hardworking, honest and well-respected man. He kept to himself and caused no trouble. He earned a good living and was tight with his money.

In the late fall of 1883, a stranger entered his horse barn and bludgeoned him with a blunt instrument. Blood was spattered all over the horse's hay and the walls of the barn. The killer stole what money Wolf had on him, then helped himself to whatever he found of value inside Wolf's home. Thinking Wolf was dead, he threw a pile of bloody hay on top of his victim. Then the stranger helped himself to a riding bridle and one of Wolf's two horses and rode away. The horse was a beautiful, athletic dark bay with a black mane and tail.

The next day, a neighbor named E. Sanford came to Wolf's farm to retrieve a square and hand saw he had loaned Wolf. When he entered the residence, he was alarmed by the disarray of bloody clothes all over the house. He found Wolf in his bed, partially clothed, with his face pounded to a pulp and blood everywhere. "Who did this to you?" he asked Wolf. "Nobody did," was his strange answer. Both his eyes were blackened and swollen shut. He was probably suffering from a concussion as well.

A local Milbank farmer, thirty-year-old Albert Wolf, was bludgeoned to death in his barn (like the one pictured) in 1883. Although the bloody iron bar used as a weapon was found, Wolf's killer was never arrested. *Courtesy of LOC, Carol M. Highsmith, photographer, #2011635383.*

Sanford hurriedly went to get some help for poor Wolf. Doctor Spates arrived and examined Wolf. The men decided to move him out of the bloody crime scene and take him to Sanford's house. Sanford cared for Wolf for almost a week, but sadly, Wolf succumbed to his wounds and died. His body was moved to the courthouse in Milbank for the inquest.

When the police investigated Wolf's barn, they discovered the bloody hay and also found a bloody piece of iron that had been wrapped in a sheet of the local newspaper. There was so much blood in the barn that it was obvious the struggle had occurred there and that Wolf had been lying in his own blood for some time before slowly making his way into his small home.

They had found the murder weapon, but unfortunately, in 1883, there was no way to use modern-day forensics like DNA testing or even fingerprint analysis. Police had very few clues to go on to find the killer.

Wolf had muttered the name "Livingston" while he was alive. Was this his killer? The only Livingstone the men knew was a man named George, who briefly worked for Sanford. When the police questioned George, he said he barely knew Wolf. The only other clue Wolf gave the police before he died was the fact that he did not know his attacker. So how could it be George?

It was also found that Wolf had hired a crew of men to thresh his wheat crop for him. Could one of these hired men have discovered that Wolf had money and planned the robbery and killing?

Another possibility is that someone saw Wolf leave Milbank with a hefty sum of money after he completed his trading the Monday of his assault. Did someone follow him home from town with the hopes of robbing him of his fortune?

The coroner revealed that Wolf was attacked so violently that the weapon had left a one-inch hole in his skull and other areas of his head were also fractured.

Wolf's killer was never found. It would be no wonder if poor Woolf was haunting Milbank, still seeking revenge for his untimely death—another unsolved murder in Milbank.

Big Stone

Founded in the 1880s as a result of the expansion of railroads into the area known as Big Stone, the town served as a productive hub for agricultural products and raw materials. In the early years, thousands of buffalo roamed the land. They enjoyed being near the water, both for quenching their thirst and for cooling their bodies during high-heat seasons. The last buffalo hunt

Unidentified passengers enjoy cruising on the beautiful *Queen of the Lake* boat on Big Stone Lake in 1899 *Courtesy of GCHS.*

was in 1879 near Stockholm, South Dakota. The hunters rounded up eight buffalo near the Strandburg area. Four were killed. History tells us that there were so many buffalo back then that one could just see a "lake of black backs" as they roamed the prairies together.

The town's name, Big Stone, derives from nearby Big Stone Lake, which was created by the construction of a dam on the Minnesota River in the 1930s. Big Stone Lake received its current name after its original Dakota Sioux name, Takojakan, was translated into English.

The historic Big Stone Hotel, built in the late 1800s, is rumored to have been visited by infamous outlaw Jesse James. While there is no concrete evidence of his stay, the legend adds an element of intrigue to the town's history.

Unsolved Deaths of Two Deaf Men

Two deaf men were tragically killed in Big Stone City, and their murderers were never found. They say the restless souls of the two young men still walk up and down the railroad tracks where their bodies were found—forever seeking revenge.

On May 22, 1913, the grisly discovery of the dead men rocked the small community. A working railroad crew discovered the first body. Later, conductor Charles Flett noticed that his Engine No. 8052 had blood and debris on it when it arrived at the depot in Milbank, South Dakota, ten miles away. This alerted him immediately to a possible tragedy.

Back in Big Stone, the train crew noticed blood on the railroad tracks and a man's bloody hat caught in the draw bar of a train. Soon, the mangled body of a young man was found just east of the brickyard in Big Stone City. The headless body was taken to Emmanuel Undertaking in Milbank. The poor fellow's head was found the next day.

The next morning, the body of a second man was found. He, too, was discovered near the railroad tracks down an embankment, by employees of the Gold & Co. Brickyard in Big Stone. His remains were taken to Ortonville, Minnesota, just a few miles away.

Coroners determined that the two men were Leslie Yaerger, age twenty-one, who came down on a Great Northern train from Canada for a baseball game in Milbank. The other man found was thirty-year-old William Messner.

When police investigated the train crew, they learned that conductor William Schmitz left Milbank around 8:05 p.m. heading toward Odessa. The train arrived in Big Stone about 8:45 p.m., so the tragedy would have

In 1913, the body of a young man was found just east of the brickyard in Big Stone City. *Courtesy of Deb Wiik, Big Stone City.*

taken place around that time. They also believed that foul play was involved. H.A. LeRoy had known Messner for two and a half years and had even learned sign language from him. He knew for a fact that Messner would never walk on the railroad tracks, as he was unable to hear the oncoming trains. Messner always wore a gold watch and chain and typically carried about eighty dollars in cash on him. Was robbery the motive?

Another railroad employee, Alex Ely, was convinced there were signs of a struggle at the scene. Both Messner and Yaerger were strong young men and met their untimely and unfortunate deaths at the hands of an unknown assailant. The killers were never arrested, and the murders were never solved.

Some claim to have seen the shadowy figure of a man near the old site of the brickyard and railroad tracks late at night. Is this one of the spirits of either Yaerger or Messner?

Murders and violent acts can trap emotions in the form of energy, creating strange occurrences that continue to happen for many years, sometimes centuries. Odors, shadows, knocking sounds, unexplained smoke and perfumes and objects moving on their own are all signs of ghostly activity.

Unsolved Murder of an Unknown Victim

Do victims of unsolved violent crimes linger on in the form of ghosts with the hope of the crime being solved so that they can finally move on to heaven in peace? Many people believe this is why spirits remain in buildings or at certain sites.

One such unsolved murder was committed in the spring of 1925, just a few miles from Big Stone City. A local farmer, Henry Bengen, was wandering the fields searching for a lost calf when he made the grisly discovery of the body of a man near the west side of the creek. He had been there for some time, as the water had made a depression around his body.

Flock & Van Stralen Undertaking in Milbank took responsibility for the corpse. They believed the victim had been killed in late fall and not discovered until spring. Coroner and doctor F.N. Cliff inspected the skeleton and discovered the man had been beaten over the head, resulting in a fractured skull. They also found that the man had been shot in the head, with a large-caliber weapon. The body had then been dragged by the feet to the spot where it was found. Robbery may or may not have been the motive, as the body still had seventy dollars and some change on it. Since the money was found in the victim's underwear, they deduced the victim may have feared being robbed, and the killer had simply failed to find the hidden money.

Bengen told the police officers that he had found a jacket earlier near the Whetstone bridge, and although it had blood on the sleeves, he did not think much about it.

Several people were missing from the area, but none matched the body's characteristics. The coroner thought the man was about fifty-five years old; he was 170 pounds and about five feet, nine inches tall.

Why did this unknown victim get killed? What was the motive? Why did the murderer both bludgeon and shoot the man? There must have been some sort of anger motive.

The identity of the body was never discovered. The killer (or killers) was never punished. This is the perfect catalyst for a vengeful ghost.

Note: In the year 2006, a whopping forty-thousand-plus unidentified bodies were reported in the United States alone, and another four-thousand-plus are added to this count every year. There are countless stories of victims who are never identified and their killers never caught.

In 1925, an unidentified corpse was found by local farmer Henry Bengen near Whetstone bridge near Big Stone City. *Courtesy of Deb Wiik, Big Stone City.*

ABERDEEN MURDERS AND GHOSTS

A Quadruple Murder

Nothing can conjure up a good ghost story better than a horrific murder. They say that the energy trapped within the walls of a crime scene can linger on for years if not cleansed away and the spirit released from the tragedy. Many ghosts hang around watching to see if their killer gets caught and prosecuted. If not, they stay on Earth with the hopes of getting the attention of a living person to help solve the crime.

One such incident occurred in 1909 in Aberdeen, South Dakota. The Christie family lived on a farm just outside of town. Emil Victor (1890–1909) was a shifty young man from New York. He decided he wanted to rob the Christies, so he snuck into their home and began stealing jewelry and other valuables.

Mr. J.W. Christie, a local grain buyer, surprised Emil when he came home, and Emil shot him dead. When his wife and his daughter Mildred (age nineteen) stumbled upon the tragedy, Emil shot them, too. An employee of the farm, Michael Ronayne, came across the grisly scene—and he was also killed by Emil.

EMIL VICTOR

In 1909, Emil Victor committed a horrific quadruple murder. He was captured and arrested in Aberdeen wearing his victim's expensive jewelry. *Drawing courtesy of author, based on a photo originally published in the* Sioux City (IA) Journal, *November 17, 1909.*

Emil fled the blood-soaked house. Neighbors alerted police that they had heard gunshots. A posse was formed and began tracking down the perpetrator. He was located a week later outside of Aberdeen as someone noted that he was wearing expensive jewelry. Again, the police were alerted. They quickly arrested Emil. He confessed to the quadruple murder and was locked up in a Brown's County solitary confinement cell.

Judge McNulty decided no appeals would be granted and warned Emil's lawyer of such, even though his lawyer was pleading temporary insanity. Emil whiled away his days eating heartily the free food granted him and playing cards with the guards.

Emil Victor's final words were, "May God forgive my sins and bless you all." He was hanged right afterward from a rope like one pictured. *Courtesy of LOC, 1865, #2008661692.*

After a brief trial, Judge McNulty announced, "It is the judgment of the court that on the sixteenth day of November 1909, you suffer death and according to the law you will be hanged by the neck until you are dead!"

Emil seemed to take the sentence coolly. His father, a successful dry goods merchant in Buffalo, New York, could do nothing to save his son from his fate. It had become known that Emil had already been arrested for beating a man and committing highway robbery. He also had shot a young boy in the head in East Aurora, New York. He had a few cases of horse theft under his belt, too. He was not going to get much sympathy from a jury or a judge. Emil Victor's fate was sealed. He was found guilty and received the death sentence in July that same year for his crazed actions.

At seven o'clock in the morning on November 16, Emil was given his last breakfast. Reverend F.J. Graeber read Emil his final rights and consoled him. The gallows were constructed, and interested citizens gathered around to watch the hanging.

"Do you have any final words?" Emil was asked.

"May God forgive my sins and bless you all."

At precisely eight o'clock, a black hood was pulled over Emil's head. Sheriff John Anderson was in charge of releasing the trap door that dropped Emil's body down nine feet of rope. He died instantly from a broken neck. At 8:10 a.m., Emil was announced dead.

Does Emil's restless soul still linger at the spot of his hanging? Do the tragic souls of the Christie family still reside where their lives were taken so ruthlessly? If the Christie farm is still standing, would the angry spirits of those killed so ruthlessly haunt the home to this day?

Residual energy can often linger in buildings and at sites where tragedies have occurred, which is what many believe creates ghosts and hauntings.

A Birthday Murder

Nothing will drum up a persistent ghost more than a horrific, ruthless murder. One such killing took place in the early morning hours in an Aberdeen apartment on May 14, 1965.

The sad spirit of a young woman named Arlene Johnson (age twenty-five) possibly remains hopeful that people may remember her. Her unsettling death was written into history by numerous accounts of her killer's trial in the newspapers. He husband, Tyrone Junior Johnson (age twenty-four), savagely beat her the night prior to her death.

The evening started out with Arlene's desire to celebrate her birthday with friends that Friday night. Another couple came over to the Johnsons' apartment; their live-in babysitter, Jeaneva Deer with Horns (age nineteen), had agreed to watch the Johnsons' three children so the two couples could enjoy a night of partying. Jeaneva had no idea this would be Arlene's last night to be alive. She had only been employed by the Johnson family for a week.

The night went from terrible to worse. The couples began drinking heavily. Tyrone was a violent man and prone to abusing Arlene. The night of the killing, Arlene had a little too much to drink—or so Tyrone said. But his lies soon came out into the open, once he knew he was caught red-handed.

Tyrone claimed that the couples were drinking at their apartment. After their friends left, Arlene went into the bathroom, where she fell and "hit her head repeatedly" on the tub due to the fact that she was tipsy. Tyrone helped her get into the bathtub to try to "sober her up," then went into another room to sleep. He had "no idea" his wife would soon be dead. He waltzed into the sheriff's office at 9:20 next morning after he found Arlene stone cold in her bed.

The police and the coroner rushed to the couple's apartment hoping to rescue Arlene, but it was indeed too late. Arlene was lying in her bed when the authorities found her lifeless body. The coroner, Doctor William Sweeny, determined that Arlene's death had been felonious and caused by a brutal beating and lack of oxygen due to a ruptured windpipe. Obviously, Tyrone was lying.

Tyrone was promptly arrested without bail. In jail, he began to get nervous. He claimed he did not even remember hitting Arlene. But her body told another story. She had multiple bruises all over her body when she was found. Tyrone claimed she had repeatedly "bumped into the furniture" while she was intoxicated.

Of course, Tyrone pleaded innocent. His defense was that Arlene's fatal injuries were due to her falling in the bathtub. He also wanted the jury members to consider the events that led up to her murder. On the witness stand, Tyrone began to crumble. He even threw in a few tears, hoping to win the jurors' sympathy. They were not buying it.

Then his story changed again during his interrogation in the courtroom. Next, he stated that he suddenly remembered hitting his wife, pulling her by the hair and beating her repeatedly with a toilet plunger until the handle broke.

Carlyle Richards, deputy state attorney, represented the deceased. Richards simply told the jury, "Johnson's story of being innocent is unreasonable, incredible and unbelievable."

Judge Philo Hall was beginning to see the truth about that fateful evening.

Again, Tyrone's story changed. The seven men and five women of the jury felt zero sympathy for Tyrone.

When asked for the truth again, Tyrone stated, "In the morning, I went into the bedroom where Arlene was sleeping. I touched her foot. It was cold. I said, 'Get up, Arlene, you have got to go to work.' (Arlene had worked for the Aberdeen Country Club.) Then I went into the kitchen and told Jeaneva Deer with Horns, 'I think Arlene is dead.'"

Jeaneva was called to the stand as the key witness. "I was in the apartment that night and the following morning. I heard the sounds of a beating just before dawn," she stated.

So why didn't she call the police? Why did she ignore the sounds of Tyrone beating poor Arlene? Was she afraid he would beat her, too? What were the three children doing during this time? Was Jeaneva preoccupied with protecting the children, as well, from Tyrone's awful behavior? Certainly, after only being in the household for a week, she had no idea what she had gotten herself into.

After a short deliberation, the jurors came to a verdict. Tyrone was convicted of second-degree manslaughter. In 1965, this sentence came with the penalty of life in prison in the state penitentiary at hard labor.

Unfortunately for Arlene, Tyrone only served four years. Hopefully, Arlene's angry spirit haunted Tyrone until his death.

HECLA

The Boxcar Murders

They say the ghost of Lee Zooks still seeks revenge for his gruesome and ruthless murder in 1905.

The day started out as a normal one. Ten friends were riding the Chicago & Northwestern passenger train heading from Aberdeen on to Hecla. The men were enjoying a casual lunch of sandwiches and beer. Working men, they took pride in being good providers and employees. Four scruffy-looking strangers boarded the train, making the group nervous. Hoping to avoid any

The ghost of Lee Zooks still seeks revenge for his gruesome and ruthless murder in 1905, which took place on a train like the one pictured. *Courtesy of LOC, 1900, #99614495.*

conflict, the men offered sandwiches to them, of which they partook. Hoping their generosity was enough to deter any problems from the scoundrels, the group held their breath until the four men debarked.

The train slowly arrived in Hecla that night without incident. But just minutes before it stopped at the depot, two masked men jumped into the car, demanding the ten men hold up their hands and give them all their valuables. Terrified, five of the men took a dangerous leap from the still-moving train. As the remaining men pulled whatever money they could from their pockets, the villains began shooting for no apparent reason.

Two of the men bravely fought their attackers. The robbers began hitting the men with the butts of their revolvers. Soon, the semi-muffled sound of a gunshot rang through the car, and one of the workers fell to the ground. The robbers, acknowledging what they just did, fled from the passenger car. The fallen man was bleeding profusely from his head. He had been robbed of ten dollars—a meager sum for a man's life.

The five men who hopped off the train at the first sign of a problem had no idea their friends had been injured and one violently killed. They telegraphed the train depot agent in Ludden, North Dakota, on the morning of September 5, requesting their luggage be held there for retrieval. They secured lodging for the night at the nearby Arlington Hotel. Little did they know the robbers had secured the night in the very same hotel.

The next morning, they heard the terrible news. Sheriff Wilmsen was notified by another guest that a suspicious-looking man was also in the hotel. Wilmsen promptly located and arrested the stranger.

The five men left together, off to board a train to ride up to Hecla to get their belongings, then onward to Oakes, North Dakota, where they joined the remaining four men. All were ordered to return to Hecla to identify the man being held on suspicion. The nine men did as they were told and positively identified the robber as the killer.

At Ludden, the train pulled into the depot. The conductor was made aware of the man lying, so close to death, on the floor of the passenger train. He notified the village constable of the dire situation. The constable quickly made his way to the car to investigate the injured man. A considerable amount of time had passed since the shooting and the arrival at Ludden.

The sight of the man was horrible, as his head had been partially blown off and his eyes were protruding from their sockets. His clothes were wet with blood, and his throat had a deep gash in it. The poor man was desperately clinging to life. All he could whisper was, "I am killed."

The conductor and constable thought it best to get the man to Oakes as quickly as possible to obtain medical attention. When the train pulled up, Doctor Boardman was waiting. He immediately did everything he could do for the dying man in the hopes of saving his life. When they realized the man would not live, the officials tried to pry whatever valuable information they could out of him before he died. He slowly told them he had a wife and children living in Morrisville, Missouri. He said his name was Lee Zooks. Then he took his last breath.

The man being held on suspicion was William Barker, and he was moved to Aberdeen for questioning. Barker had just been released from a three-year stint in jail for assault with the intent to kill and was known as an extremely dangerous man. Somehow, he'd managed to get out of jail on good behavior.

Three unknown hoodlums showed up at the jail where Barker was being held, thinking they could break Barker free from his cell, but the police asked them to leave the premises. Barker was then told he was being charged with the murder of Zooks. He did not appear to be surprised.

Barker was kept behind bars until his trial, which was scheduled for December. The jury took a little less than an hour to find Barker guilty of murder. His punishment would be life with hard labor at the state penitentiary at Sioux Falls.

Lee Zook's life was tragically taken at age twenty over just a few bucks, leaving his wife and child without a husband and father. If his restless spirit is still wandering this earth in the hopes of seeking revenge, it would be warranted.

THE SKULLS OF HURON

In a downtown office in Huron during the chilly winter month of February 1963, a local electrician was shocked as he went about his daily job. Merlin Horsted was hired to do a little electrical work in the upstairs office located at 126 Third Street Southwest in town. Boy, was he shocked when he discovered two human skulls inside the walls!

Horrified, he contacted the local police immediately. Chief of police for Huron Martin Molter rushed to the scene. Molter packed up the two skulls and took them to the coroner for examination. Looking at the skulls, he found that the skull of victim no. 1 had suffered a puncture wound inflicted by a blunt object or, possibly, a bullet. The skull of victim no. 2

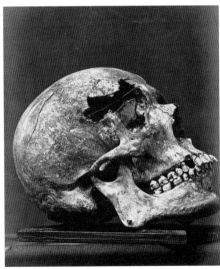

The skulls (similar to these pictured) of two murder victims were found by electrician Merlin Horsted hidden inside the walls in an office in Huron. *Courtesy of LOC, War Department, Surgeon General's Office, #2005696470.*

did not have any visible marks on it. Both skulls were missing their teeth and lower jawbones. The sheriff determined that the men had obviously met with foul play.

Back at the police office, Molter searched his records for any missing persons reported in the area. None were logged. So who did these two skulls belong to? Where were their bodies? Who murdered them? Why did they remove their skulls and keep them inside the walls?

The current office owners did not have any information pertaining to the identity of the skulls and were as shocked as the electrician and police. No further information can be found about the follow-up to this case.

Do the restless souls of these two murdered people still seek answers about their untimely deaths? It is quite common for murder victims to hang around the scene of the crime as ghostly apparitions. Do they seek justice? Revenge?

UNIDENTIFIED FLYING OBJECTS AND GHOSTS

South Dakota is known for its hundreds of sightings of unexplained phenomena. Dating as far back as 1874, residents have been puzzled by unknown objects in the sky. Some believe these are aliens from outer space; others believe the objects are flown by supernatural beings from another dimension. It is estimated that around 350 unusual sightings have been logged—but how many more incidents have gone unrecorded? In South Dakota, a surprising increase in these phenomena began around 1947.

Could paranormal beings control these strange objects? How can they manipulate time, energy and light in much the same manner ghosts do? Ghosts can somehow make objects move, manipulate light and shadows, make items appear and disappear, create smoke or perfume odors and so much more. UFOs are often seen clearly with the naked eye, much as ghosts are, and then magically disappear in a blink—just like ghosts.

Perhaps the world is being misled into thinking that unidentified flying objects are being controlled by little green men from outer space? Maybe they are not aliens at all but instead light beings or ghosts. Would that explain why the drivers of these craft can never be caught or properly recorded?

The first sighting in South Dakota was recorded by Annie Tallent, a member of the Gordon Party, which came to the Black Hills in 1874. After she experienced the strange lights in the sky, she wrote in her diary:

About noon, on a clear, chilly day, an awful rushing, roaring sound was heard above and to the north of us. It was almost directly over our camp. Everyone immediately looked in that direction and saw an object rushing through the air from east to west, not more than one-half mile above the treetops, and seemingly not more than three quarters of a mile distant from us. It seemed almost white and looked at least as if it might be 30- or 40-feet diameter, although its size could not be ascertained with any degree of accuracy. As it seemed surrounded with steam or smoke, it did not appear to be falling but continued in a horizontal course. Three or four seconds after having passed out of our sight to the west, a report was heard that fairly shook the Hills, while its track clouds of smoke were left that could be seen for 20 minutes after. It was the grandest sight I had ever witnessed.... There was one thing that was very evident: immediately after this sighting, the weather began to grow colder, and continued to increase in intensity each day for about three weeks.

Since the Wright brothers would not invent their airplane until 1903, there's no reasonable explanation for Tallent observing anything of that nature in the skies of South Dakota in 1874.

As far back as 1897, the town of Brookings has been a hot spot for unusual activity. A man named S.E. Hayden was shocked one morning when he looked up into the sky and watched a strange craft slam into a nearby windmill at Judge Proctor's house. He ran to investigate and was scared to death when he came across some sort of being "not from this world." The town retrieved the unworldly being and gave it a Christian burial in the small town of Aurora, near Brookings. Since then, many have wanted to dig up the strange being in order to determine what exactly it was, but the idea has not been well received by locals. Perhaps if the body of the being were exhumed, it would offer clues about the strange pilot of the craft. But for now, it remains an unsolved mystery.

In 1956, strange objects, lights and rapidly moving fireballs were reported in many South Dakota towns, such as Rapid City, Redfield, Mobridge, McLaughlin, Lemmon, Aberdeen, Pierre, Mitchell, Martin and Hot Springs.

In the year 1960, people reported multiple sightings of strange light beams, bright streaks, fast-moving orbs and other strange objects in the skies of South Dakota. Credible airline pilots reported unusual objects glowing and moving at unusual speeds near the Sioux Falls area.

Brookings, South Dakota, still tends to be a hot spot for unusual objects hovering in the sky. In 2018, a video of an odd saucer-type object, almost translucent, was captured. The strange circle of light remained in the sky for over an hour. The exact same object was recorded again in the same spot the following year.

In March 2022, four large disk-type objects were seen changing in size and eventually growing larger until they simply disappeared. This occurrence lasted for approximately seven minutes. That same month, an unusual ball of light, or orb, was filmed in Brookings.

Orbs are often considered evidence of a ghostly spirit in paranormal investigations and are easily captured on film. But what if these light orbs, of a significantly greater size, also travel outside in the open air? What's to limit them to being inside a building? Perhaps because investigators focus on spirits roaming indoors, they are forgetting the possibility of spirits out in the fresh air.

The National U.F.O. Reporting Center has now logged 382 unidentified objects in the state of South Dakota. In the northeastern section of the state, there have been many remarkable claims reported, such as:

- September 17, 2022, Aberdeen: A fireball floated around for hours, then slowly faded.
- June 26, 2022, Wilmot: A pilot observed two spherical objects flying in formation below his aircraft that appeared for about ten seconds.
- March 15, 2022, Brookings: Four disks appeared, got bigger and bigger, then eventually disappeared. The sighting lasted seven minutes, fifteen seconds.
- March 2, 2022, Brookings: A ball of light accelerated overhead into the distance.
- December 5, 2020, Huron: A line of moving lights hovered in the sky for three minutes.
- July 27, 2020, Brookings: A cirular object, brown in color, was seen traveling around thirty-five to forty miles per hour.
- April 18, 2020, Milbank: A strand of white lights that lasted about fifteen to thirty minutes was seen.
- April 8, 2019, Brookings: A sighting of a triangular object with seven lights on the bottom, appearing to be a few hundred feet from the ground, lasted several minutes.
- May 26, 2018, Gary: For five minutes, ten bright orange lights moved into formation, hovered, turned white and then vanished.

- November 13, 2014, Huron: Two separate reports were made of a very big triangular UFO and another of three glowing red lights.
- August 19, 2014, Watertown: A sighting of a bright, cool blue flashing object moving erratically, like a bug, lasted four minutes.
- December 27, 2013, Corona: Three triangular light forms that appeared white, blue and green flashed across the sky quickly and silently.

What exactly are these strange light objects in our skies? Some think they are light beings or angels; others are certain they are aliens or monsters. Are the occurrences getting more and more frequent, or is it simply that people are becoming more comfortable admitting to seeing unidentified objects? The mystery continues.

MILLER

Mail-Order Romeo Hides in Miller

The small, quiet town of Miller, South Dakota, is located in Hand County. Its population is under 1,500 people. Founded in 1881, the town was named after Mr. Henry Miller.

In 1924, the town became home to a ruthless killer named Harm Drenth (1893–1932), known to Miller residents as Joseph Gildow, a.k.a. Harry Powers and Cornelius Pierson. Drenth kept to himself, and the only permanent detail about his residence there was his rented post office box. Police discovered after his arrest that he had rented access to box 13 in Miller for a very grisly and deadly reason.

Clueless they even had a killer in their mist, locals continued their lives as usual, never worrying about whether a killer would uproot any of their lives with the flash of a knife. Once the details about his murders came out in the newspapers, Miller residents were in shock. How could such a monster live among them so quietly? So undetected? The horrific details of the way their fellow citizen killed his prisoners were gasp-worthy indeed. Concerned citizens of Miller later worried that a few missing persons from their area may have fallen victim to Drenth.

Drenth had turned himself into a mail-order Romeo. He would write pen pal style letters to unsuspecting women all over the United States.

Serial killer Harm Drenth (a.k.a. Harry Powers) lured women by writing them love letters then killing them for their money. *Courtesy of the Dayton, Ohio police; mug shot taken in 1920.*

How did he find his prey? He drummed up extensive and elaborate claims about owning his own matrimonial agency, but in actuality, it was a fake mail-order matchup scheme, one that he used only for himself. He would write long, detailed letters about love, home life, happiness—all the things so many women want. It was reported that twenty letters per day came flooding into Drenth's post office box, all from lonely women looking for love. Drenth had an unusual tactic: coding his letters with odd numbers and letters (later to be deciphered by authorities). In one case, he had written "216" under the stamp. Code experts and authorities translated the numbers to the word *graveyard*. He obviously intended to kill this unlucky woman.

But several women, one with three innocent children, would soon become his targets. One of possibly many victims was Mrs. Asta Buick Eicher, a widow from Park Ridge, Illinois. She was raising several children and longed for another husband to help with them. She began writing to Mr. "Cornelius Orvin Pierson" in the hopes of getting married. He (Pierson/Drenth) wooed her (along with countless other women) until he had her trapped in his trance of love.

Unfortunately, Asta would not find love. (Drenth was already married to a woman named Luella.) He wanted Asta's money, not her romance. She lived in a nice house—but little did he know that Asta was in financial ruin and worried about her children's welfare and education. Her mortgage was weighing heavily on her, as well as unpaid taxes. When Drenth discovered he would not be marrying into money, he decided to kill her. But he did not stop there. He decided to kill her three children as well.

On June 23, 1931, Drenth showed up at Asta's door to sweep her off her feet. He told the nanny, Elizabeth Abernathy, that he and Asta were going to set up their new home together and return for the children.

A few days passed. Suddenly, a letter arrived from Asta saying that Drenth would come to retrieve the children, Grete (age fifteen), Harry (age twelve) and Annabelle (age eleven). When Drenth arrived, he said they were all going on a family vacation together to Europe, so they would be gone for some time. But before their departure, he handed one of the children a check to cash at the bank. The teller at the bank recognized the signature on the check as false and refused to cash it.

Angry, Drenth left empty-handed, except for the three children in tow. He took the children back to a makeshift murder den in the basement of a farm he rented from his real wife, Luella, in Quiet Dell, West Virginia. What took place there is too horrible to imagine. Their mother was bound, unable to escape the sound-proof basement. The children were tossed into the room as well, unable to escape.

It is unclear whether Drenth left the locked doors of his dungeon to round up another victim, Dorothy Pressler Lemke, or if that was later. (When he confessed, he told police he killed them all on the same day, but following the stories in newspapers, it is believed he met up with Dorothy a few days later.)

Dorothy was fifty years old. She knew Drenth as D.P. Lowther. He had convinced her that they would be moving to his ranch in Cedar Rapids, Iowa. He also convinced her to pawn all her valuables for cash and drain her bank accounts of $4,000.

Dorothy Lemke (*pictured*) was one of mail-order Romeo Harm Drenth's many victims. He had her drain her bank accounts of $4,000 before killing her. *Drawing courtesy of author.*

When they went to ship Dorothy's trunk to their new "home," she noticed it was being sent to "Cornelius O. Pierson" of Fairmont, West Virginia. That is when she should have run away. But she did not. She continued to believe her knight in shining armor was there to rescue her. Instead, he took her to his murder chamber.

The world knows only the grisly details that surfaced in Drenth's confession after he was captured. He told police that he took the captives one by one from the basement and led them into various rooms, where he had ropes hanging. There he strangled them all, one after the other. After they were dead, he bashed their heads with a hammer. Drenth especially tortured poor young Harry. He made him watch as he killed his mother, and when Harry started screaming, Drenth bashed his skull in.

In August, the police began investigating the disappearance of Asta and her children. When they arrived at her home, they found Drenth robbing the place clean. He was promptly arrested (this time for good, as in 1919, he had escaped from a Wisconsin jail where he was being held on burglary charges). When the police searched his farmhouse in Quiet Dell, they were horrified to find blood, hair, a child's footprint and a partially burned bank book.

Locals soon heard about the murders and began gathering around the Quiet Dell farm. A fifteen-year-old boy believed he had something to tell the authorities: he had been hired to dig a long ditch on the property. He led them to the ditch, where men began to dig. There, they found the bodies of all five victims.

Police began to suspect that Drench had been involved in other murders. On May 10, 1928, a carpet sweeper named Dudley C. Wade mysteriously disappeared. Wade worked with Drenth at a carpet-sweeping company in Adamston, West Virginia. Soon after Wade disappeared, Drenth took over as manager of the company. Things started to look suspicious to company officials and the local police, as carpet sweepers were going missing as well. When police searched Drenth's garage on Lynn Avenue in Broad Oaks, West Virginia, they found it full of stolen sweepers. Drenth's lame excuse was that Wade had been stealing them and Drenth was collecting them to return to the store. Drenth was arrested, but at his trial, his ridiculous excuse won over the jurors. He was released. To add salt to the wound, Drenth sued the sweeper company and received a reward. It is hard to swallow that had Drenth gone to prison for the theft, perhaps he would have confessed to Wade's murder, committing him to jail and therefore resulting in the lives of many being saved, in the future, from certain death. Did Wade and Drenth get into some sort of scuffle, infuriating Drenth to the point of murder? Wade's body was never found, and his fate remains a mystery.

Another unsolved murder, that of a Jane Doe found in Morris, Illinois, was mysteriously linked to Drenth. A woman from whom Drenth formerly rented a garage recognized him in photographs in the paper after his capture. Horrified, she told the police that, years ago, a disgusting odor had been oozing from the garage. When she mentioned this to the renter, he seemed agitated. A few days later, the decomposing body of a woman, wrapped in burlap, was found lying next to a highway near Morris. Did Drenth quickly remove the corpse and dump it on the side of the road? Most likely.

After his final capture, when the police asked Drenth *exactly* how many people he had killed, he calmly said, "I don't know."

The thought of someone so brutally sadistic living among various communities is truly frightening. Murder victims sometimes linger at their murder sites in the hopes of seeing their killer get penalized for the crime. In this case, any or all lingering ghosts of those who met an untimely death at Drenth's hands most certainly would want justice. If they did hang around, they would at least be happy to know justice was served.

Drenth tried to avoid conviction by claiming he was temporarily insane, but that trick did not work on the jurors or the judge. His killings were so well planned that there could have been nothing "temporary" about them. Judge John Southern sentenced him to death by hanging; his execution was scheduled for March 18, 1932. When Drenth's lawyer, J. Ed Law, tried to get the sentence changed (claiming Drenth did not get his rights read to him properly), the judge simply said, "I have no changes to my original ruling." Law then tried to stall the execution by demanding a last-minute stay. That did not work either.

On March 18, just as scheduled, Drenth walked alone up the thirteen steps of the gallows (constructed in the local opera house due to limited space in the usual hanging spot) where he would meet his fate. When he was asked if he had any last words, he said, "No."

The chaplain in attendance said, "We commit Harry Powers's soul to Thee and ask that Thou pardon his sins."

Drenth smiled at the forty-two witnesses, the police officers, the chaplain and everyone else within eyesight. At precisely nine o'clock in the morning, Deputy E. C. Brill, captain of the prison guards, signaled for the black hood to be placed over Drenth's head, the noose tightened and the drop performed. Three men all pushed their buttons simultaneously (so none would know who was responsible for the drop).

The trapdoor under Drenth's feet opened, flinging the prisoner to his death. But death was not instant. Drenth hung there for an agonizing eleven

Drenth hung from the noose from a scaffold similar to one pictured for an agonizing eleven minutes until he was finally pronounced dead. Some felt that was justice for his crimes. *Courtesy of LOC, Carol M. Highsmith, photographer, #2018663067.*

minutes until he was finally pronounced dead. His handwritten, signed confession was found later in his cell. He felt no remorse for his actions but believed his trial was unfair and that the public had ridiculed him.

Drenth's widow, Luella, claimed he was innocent right up until the end, but she did not claim his body after he was hanged.

The citizens of Miller, South Dakota, dodged a bullet when it came to Drenth's wrath. But they will never know if Drenth did kill some of their own and got away with murder—literally.

NOTE: For a more detailed story about Drenth and pictures of him and some of his victims please read "Women in Killer Powers' Life," by Ruth Reynolds, *Daily News Sun*, November 1, 1931.

In Conclusion

Haunted places and the presence of ghosts in our lives and imaginations serve as a reminder of the bizarre connection between the distant past and the present. These mysterious places, whether old houses, dense forests or unusual landscapes, disclose legends, retold stories and strong emotions that refuse to fade away.

Unbelievable tales beckon us to explore the boundaries of reality, sparking curiosity about the mysteries that lie beyond what we can see with our eyes and fully understand to be real. Haunted places and the ghosts that inhabit them evoke a sense of wonder, inviting us to ponder the thin veil between the known and the unknown and the timeless tales that continue to shape our perception of the world and the afterlife.

Keep your eyes and ears open, my friends, and hopefully you will experience a real-life haunting for yourself!

BIBLIOGRAPHY

Benedict, Adam. "Cryptid Profile: The Thunder Horse." Pine Barrens Institute, August 19, 2018. https://pinebarrensinstitute.com/.

Ferguson, Lawrence. "An Unknown Menace Puzzles Cattlemen." *Rapid City (SD) Journal*, October 23, 1977.

Gevik, Brian. "The Ghost of Watertown's Goss Opera." South Dakota Public Broadcasting, October 22, 2020. https://www.sdpb.org/.

History in South Dakota (blog). "Women in Business, Milbank 1909." January 21, 2021. https://historysouthdakota.wordpress.com/.

Johnson, Norma. *Wagon Wheels*. Sisseton, SD: Courier, 1981.

Kulkar, Kerry. "Watertown's Paranormal Society Ghost Hunts." Watertown Public Opinion, October 31, 2002.

McLaughlin, James. "An Account of Sitting Bull's Death." Philadelphia, PA: Office of Indian Rights Association, 1891. Scanned by North Dakota State University. http://heritagerenewal.org.

Osborne, Terri. "Scary House on the Prairie: Laura Ingalls Wilder's Brush With 'Bloody Benders' Serial Killers." Investigation Discovery, August 2, 2017. https://www.investigationdiscovery.com.

South Dakota Historical Society Foundation. "Nearly 150 years of Recorded UFO Sightings across South Dakota." September 4, 2021; updated October 9, 2022. https://www.capjournal.com/.

Tonsfeldt, Ali. "Ghosts of Fort Sisseton." South Dakota Game, Fish & Parks. October 8, 2019. https://gfp.sd.gov/.

Websites

Haunted Rooms America. https://www.hauntedrooms.com.
Historical Marker Database. https://www.hmdb.org.
Legends of America. https://www.legendsofamerica.com.
Mutual UFO Network (MUFON). https://mufon.com.
National UFO Reports Database. https://nuforc.org.
Occult World. https://occult-world.com.
Only in Your State. https://www.onlyinyourstate.com.
The Shadowlands. http://www.theshadowlands.net.
SouthDakotaMagazine.com. https://www.southdakotamagazine.com.
Travel South Dakota. https://www.travelsouthdakota.com.

Newspapers

Aberdeen (SD) Democrat
September 8, 1905

Argus Leader (Sioux Falls, SD)
April 9, 1909
April 9, 1923
May 26, 1932
December 8, 1937
July 31, 1941
August 31, 1960
October 8, 1974
December 13, 1975
October 14 and 28, 1977
July 15, 2004

Boston Globe
August 31, 1931

Daily News (New York)
November 1, 1931

Daily Plainsman (Huron, SD)
September 3 and 8, 1931

November 12, 1931
February 10, 1963
July 16, 1965
December 10 and 12, 1965

Daily Republic (Mitchell, SD)
February 20, 1975

Deadwood (SD) Pioneer Times
March 21, 1936

Erie (KA) Record
May 10, 1895

Grant County Review (Milbank, SD)
November 15, 1883

Herald Advance (Milbank, SD)
November 23, 1883
October 16, 1885
February 12, 1886
March 23, 1906
July 8, 1910
May 30, 1913
July 17, 1914

Lead (SD) Daily Call
September 13, 1909
May 27, 1965

Morning Democrat (Davenport, IA)
November 28, 1865

News Messenger (Fremont, OH)
March 19, 1932

Rapid City (SD) Journal
March 20, 1936
August 29, 1940

November 18, 1951
May 18, 1965
July 14, 15 and 19, 1965
September 29, 1974
August 26, 1976
October 17, 1977
April 17, 1979
November 24, 1982
December 29, 1985

Saturday News (Watertown, SD)
December 18, 1908
July 30, 1909
August 6, 1909
September 10, 1909
October 8 and 22, 1909
November 19 and 26, 1909
July 22, 1910
August 5, 1910
May 29, 1913
June 26, 1913

Sioux City (IA) Journal
November 4, 1893
July 11, 1909
November 17, 1909

Sisseton (SD) Weekly Standard
June 26, 1914
June 15, 1917

Weekly News Democrat (Emporia, KS)
May 23, 1873

ABOUT THE AUTHOR

Originally from Ithaca, New York, Deborah Cuyle loves everything about the history of America's cities—large or small. Her other passions include volunteering at her local historical society, rescuing animals, exploring museums, rock hunting and horses. Deborah, her husband and her son are currently living in a crumbling haunted mansion in South Dakota, which was built in 1883. Even creepier? It was once used as a funeral home…

Also by Deborah Cuyle

Ghosts and Legends of Spokane (WA)
Ghosts of Leavenworth and the Cascade Foothills (WA)
Ghosts of Coeur d'Alene and the Silver Valley (ID)
Ghostly Tales of Coeur d'Alene (ID)
Ghostly Tales of Snohomish (WA)
Ghostly Tales of the Pacific Northwest (OR, WA and BC)
Haunted Eastern Washington (WA—coming soon!)
Haunted Snohomish (WA)
Haunted Southwest Montana (MT)
Haunted Everett (WA)
Images of Cannon Beach (OR)
Kidding Around Portland (OR)
Murder and Mayhem in Coeur d'Alene and the Silver Valley (ID)
Murder and Mayhem in Deadwood (SD—coming soon!)
Murder and Mayhem in Spokane (WA)
Wicked Coeur d'Alene (ID)
Wicked Spokane (WA)
The 1910 Wellington Disaster (WA)

FREE eBOOK OFFER

Scan the QR code below, enter your e-mail address and get our original Haunted America compilation eBook delivered straight to your inbox for free.

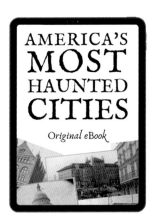

ABOUT THE BOOK

Every city, town, parish, community and school has their own paranormal history. Whether they are spirits caught in the Bardo, ancestors checking on their descendants, restless souls sending a message or simply spectral troublemakers, ghosts have been part of the human tradition from the beginning of time.

In this book, we feature a collection of stories from five of America's most haunted cities: Baltimore, Chicago, Galveston, New Orleans and Washington, D.C.

SCAN TO GET
AMERICA'S MOST HAUNTED CITIES

Having trouble scanning? Go to:
biz.arcadiapublishing.com/americas-most-haunted-cities